MW00512735

DAY TRADING OPTIONS

Quick Guide to become an Expert, Learn Various Strategies and Make More Money with Day Trading.

ROBERT MORGAN

Table of Contents

Introduction

Some time ago the main people that could trade effectively in the stock trade were individuals working for large monetary foundations, financiers, and trading houses. Be that as it may, with the advancement of the web and web trading homes, specialists have made it significantly simpler for the commonplace individual financial specialist to put resources into on the game.

Day trading can end up being an incredibly remunerating vocation, given that you do it effectively. In any case, what's more, it tends to be to some degree hard for learners - especially for individuals that aren't completely arranged with a methodology. The most experienced day vendors may arrive at unpleasant patches and ability misfortunes. Along these lines, exactly what is day trading and in what capacity would this be able to work?

KEY TAKEAWAYS

•Day vendors are occupied dealers who actualize intraday plans to increase off cost changes for a specific resource.

•Day trading utilizes a tremendous cluster of systems and strategies to benefit from apparent market wasteful aspects.

•Day trading is frequently described by particular assessment and takes a high measure of self-restraint and objectivity.

The Fundamentals of Day Trading

Day Trading is portrayed as the deal and acquisition of a security inside one trading day. It might occur in practically any market however is generally visit in the remote trade (forex) and securities trades) Day merchants are commonly accomplished and very much subsidized. They use elevated levels of influence and transient trading techniques to exploit little value developments in profoundly fluid stocks or monetary standards.

Informal investors are receptive to occasions which cause momentary market developments. Trading the data is a most loved procedure. Planned declarations like monetary measurements, organization income or loan fees are liable to advertise desires and commercial center brain research. Markets react when those desires aren't satisfied or are outperformed, as a rule with sudden, noteworthy developments, which may harvest merchants.

Informal investors use various intraday systems. These plans include:

•Scalping, that attempts to make various small gains on little costs changes during the evening

•Range trading, which generally uses opposition and bolster levels to find out their buy and sell choices

•News-based trading, which for the most part takes advantage of trading lucky breaks out of the expanded unpredictability about data occasions

•High-recurrence trading (HFT) approaches utilizing modern computations to abuse present moment or little market wasteful aspects

A Controversial Practice

The Profit plausibility of day trading is perhaps among the most discussed and misjudged issues on Wall Street. Web day trading tricks have lured novices by promising tremendous returns in a concise period. The idea that such a trading is that a supporting methodology endures. Some person's day trade without sufficient comprehension. Anyway some dealers get by even though - or possibly due to the threats.

Numerous Professional cash administrators and money related guides avoid day trading asserting that, by and large, the result doesn't warrant the hazard. On the other hand, the individuals who do evening business demand there's benefit to be made. Day trading beneficially is potential, notwithstanding, the achievement rate is decreased because of the complexity and obligatory danger of day trading mix with the related tricks. Also, business analysts and money related experts the same affirm that long spans, dynamic trading plans regularly fail to meet expectations an increasingly crucial uninvolved marker plan, especially after expenses and charges are thought about.

Day Trading isn't proper for everyone and involves huge dangers. Also, it requires an intensive appreciation of how the business sectors work and different methodologies for benefitting in the concise term. While we review the examples of overcoming adversity of people who became super wealthy as an informal investor, remember that many don't many will burn out. Most will just scarcely remain above water. Besides, don't think little of the job that karma and respectable time play. At the same time, capacity is without a doubt a segment, a defeat of awful fortune can sink even the most experienced informal investor.

Characteristics of a Day Trader

Proficient Day sellers - the individuals who trade professionally rather than as a side interest - are generally settled inside the claim to fame. They for the most part have inside and out comprehension of the market, moreover. Here are a Few of the prerequisites required for a fruitful informal investor:

Information and aptitude from the market

People who attempt to day trade with no comprehension of market essentials regularly take out cash. Specialized examination and chart perusing is a phenomenal capacity for an informal investor to get. Yet, with no more extensive appreciation of the market you are in and the assets which exist in that current market, diagrams may be misleading. Do your due perseverance and grasp the particular the inward operations of the product that you trade.

Adequate Funding

Informal investors utilize just danger capital that they may bear to lose. Does this shield them from budgetary ruin, yet also, it can help evacuate feeling out of their trading. A lot of assets is much of the time fundamental to underwrite successfully on intraday value moves. Approaching your edge records can be urgent, because unpredictable swings may acquire edge approaches short notification.

Plan

A Dealer requires an edge over the remainder of the commercial center. There are numerous one of a kind systems informal investors use, for example, swing trading, trade, and trading data. These plans are refined until they produce steady benefits and viably limit misfortunes.

Order

A Profitable methodology is pointless without subject. Numerous informal investors end up losing a lot of money since they don't make trades that satisfy their specific guidelines. As they state, "Plan the business and trade the procedure." Success is inconceivable without subject.

To Gain, informal investors depend vigorously on instability on the commercial center. A stock could be speaking to your informal investor when it moves a decent arrangement for the day. That could happen because of a scope of various things, for example, a marketing chart, financial specialist conclusion, or maybe generally monetary or business news.

Informal investors likewise favor stocks which are intensely fluid since that offers them the chance to alter their situation without changing the price tag of this stock. At the point when a stock cost goes higher, brokers may take a purchase position. If the cost goes, a vendor may pick to short-sell so he can pick up when it drops.

Notwithstanding what approach a day vendor utilizes, they are normally looking to trade a stock that moves... a ton.

Day Trading for a Living

There are two key divisions of expert informal investors: people who work autonomously or the individuals who work to get a greater foundation. Most informal investors who trade professionally work for a major organization. These vendors have an edge since they approach a rule, a trading work area, extensive amounts of influence and capital, costly logical applications, in addition to considerably more. These sellers are commonly scanning for simple benefits which might be drawn up out of trade openings and data occasions, and such apparatuses grant them to exploit those less hazardous day trades before singular dealers may react.

Singular Traders now and again handle others' cash or simply trade with their one of a kind. Not many of these approaches a trading work area, anyway they as often as possible have solid ties into some agent (in light of the enormous totals they contribute on commissions) and access to extra sources.

Then again, the constrained degree of those assets keeps them from contending legitimately with day by day vendors. Or maybe, they need to face more challenges. Singular dealers regularly trade utilizing specialized assessment and swing trades - combined with an influence - to make adequate benefits on these little value developments in profoundly fluid stocks.

Day Trading requests availability to some of the confounded budgetary administrations and devices in the market.

Informal investors normally request:

Access Into a trading work area

This is normally saved for sellers working for greater establishments or individuals who handle significant amounts of cash. The working work area furnishes these sellers with prompt buy executions, which can be particularly significant when sharp value developments occur. By method of occurrence, when a procurement is declared, informal investors considering merger trade may put in their requests until the rest of the commercial center can profit by the cost differential.

Numerous News assets

News Provides most by far of chances from that informal investors compete, along these lines it's basic to be the first to know when something significant happens. The ordinary trading region incorporates passage to the Dow Jones Newswire, ceaseless inclusion of CNBC and different news associations, and applications that consistently examines news assets for significant stories.

Expository Applications

Trading Applications is an exorbitant prerequisite for a long time brokers. Individuals who depend on specific signs or swing trades depend more on applications than data. The accompanying may recognize this PC programming:

•Automated design acknowledgment: This typically implies the trading framework recognizes specialized markers, for example, banners and stations, or substantially more convoluted pointers like Elliott Wave designs.

•Genetic and neural programming: These are applications utilizing neural systems and hereditary calculations to perfect trading frameworks to make progressively exact forecasts of future value moves.

CHAPTER 1:

What Is Day Trading?

In day trading, you get to buy and sell the underlying asset or instrument on the same day, in a way that all the positions are closed by the time the market closes in the trading day. Most of the traders that engage in day trading are speculators. The main aim at the end of each trade is to get to walk away with profits that you are happy about. Day trading is more of a short-term investment. You either walk away with a profit or a loss. It also provides a chance to take part in multiple trades. As a beginner, this may not be a good start-up strategy. You cannot be engaging in more than two trades when you do not have adequate information on how you can go about different trades. Making rushed decisions to get in trades without proper planning is like setting yourself up for failure. You know that you are going to fail, yet you proceed with the plan. Be careful to free yourself from such occurrences in life. If you are a beginner, you can start by understanding how the whole process works before committing yourself to engage in the trade.

To avoid negative price gaps resulting in the difference between the day's closing price and the next day's opening price, day traders get to exit positions before the market closes. This exit also protects them from unmanageable risks that they may not be able to tackle. Day traders utilize margin leverage while carrying out different trades. For most brokers, the acceptable leverage margin is 4:1, which can be reduced to 2:1 by the end of the day. The popular financial instruments that traders engage in include currencies, options, stocks, host of future contracts, and contracts for difference. Depending on the instrument that you find suitable, you can carry out the trade that you wish to be part of. As you decide to trade, you will require a broker, through which you can use to carry out your different trades. As you select the best broker, there are some factors that you will have to consider. As you keep reading, you will come across these factors that will guide you in getting the best broker.

Day trading is a profitable investment, and there is a lot that you can make as a trader. The different trading strategies and trading plan will help you stay on top of your game as a trader. In the book, I have tried to provide information that will help you become a better trader. I will not promise that it will be an easy journey. The steps that you take toward becoming a better trader will set you apart despite the bumps that you will come across. Anybody can make a good trader as long as they have the right attitude.

Why Trade Options?

Generate an Income

As an investor, you are looking for a venture that will generate capital for you. This goal makes you focus on opportunities that bring profits, and it helps you avoid all the factors that can expose the venture to risks that result in a loss. We have individuals who are making a fortune out of day trading. As a beginner, one of the focuses that you have is to become a master of the game. In any business, we have people that are making it and those that are struggling and barely making ends meet. The different approaches to what we are doing bring a difference in our output. Depending on how good your approach is, you can equally earn an amount that measures up to the work that you give. It is without any doubt that there are different levels for different traders in the industry. Some are at the peak of their careers where they are earning a lot. At the same time, some people are struggling with average results and barely making it. After engaging in trade, they all walk out with different incomes. The climax of a trader is getting to a point where they easily make successful trades and earn a fortune from them. Getting to this point is possible as long as you are committed to putting in the work.

Is there a limit amount in day trading? Well, people ask this to know what to expect when they get on top and become experts. I do not think that there is a limited amount that you can earn while trading options. The only limit you can have is the one that you have set individually if you decide that you only need half a million from the trades you make per month that is likely the figure that you will get at the end. At the same time, you can set some big figures that you expect to match up to, so you put in a lot of effort into ensuring that you get to the point that you aspire to get to. You ensure that you are fully devoted to hitting the target; this will see you place a lot of effort and hard work in ensuring that you get the results that you desire. We are who we choose to become. If you choose to have a limited mentality, you get average results. Alternatively, if you decide that you are not a limited edition, you stretch to further horizons and get to exceed your expectations. I choose to believe that the income one generates from day trading is not limited to certain figures. You get to decide what you are worth and chose to define who you are by making the best decisions regarding what you are doing.

Profits with Low Investment

With day trading, the profits that you collect are not limited to the investment that you make. The idea that you can only make huge profits with a big investment happens to be a myth. A good trader is not defined by how big their investment is, but rather by how well they play their cards. You find that even while gambling, the individual with more to lose does not always stand the upper chance at winning. As a gambler, you might be having very little to offer and still win the gamble. The differentiating factor at the end of the day is the strategy that you use to win the gamble. With a very good plan, you can walk away as the winner, even if you had little to offer. This also happens in life. You find that the individual who managed to take a good win home had little, yet a proper and well-structured plan got them to acquire the win among the people who had more. The plan and approach used are essential to success. It helps you find the best angle to attack the situation at hand and makes you successful at it. The idea that you need to have more to get more will not always work. With little, you can decide to turn over the situation to a more favorable outcome. The idea is not limited to the amount of revenues that you have to bring to the table; the problem should be how far you are willing to go to get what you want.

Can our expectations make us want to invest in more? Most defiantly, yes. With an ambition of wanting to become an overnight success, you might find yourself making decisions that do not go well for you. At that point, you have very big expectations of becoming a millionaire. There is a certain definition you have for success that is according to what you like and what you believe in. You find that you are willing to break your neck just to get to the point that you aspire. At times, these desires can be harmful, especially when you have very high expectations. You are likely to make wrong decisions and not take your time carefully planning your ways. To avoid finding yourself in such situations, you must learn to have a realistic approach to your goals. In this case, you get to retain the goals that you have in mind as you come up with a realistic approach to tackle different trades. As you begin, it would be best if you started with a small investment. Even as you start with small profits, you can start earning bigger profits in the future. The plan is first to get ahold of the activities that surround a trade. Identify the different factors influencing the trade as you come up with ways to make successful trades. In the end, you learn how to convert your knowledge into a sustainable income.

Insurance

We are currently in space and time, where people appreciate the need for insurance. It is always good to secure your investments from the possible risks that may arise. Different insurance companies have different insurance plans. They want to ensure that they offer services that their clients can easily relate to and buy. The benefits of having insurance are many. One of the key benefits of insurance is that it protects one from the possibility of incurring a complete loss. Supposing you purchased a gadget today, and it got broken the next day. You would have incurred a complete loss if you had not taken insurance. With insurance, you can easily get compensated for the loss. This can be done by being given another similar but used gadget or getting a new gadget. You do not incur a complete loss. Life is unpredictable. One day, you are healthy, and the next day, you are involved in a bad accident that leaves you fighting for your life. Such an event is not planned, so there may come a time when you are unable to cater to the accumulated bills. In such a situation, your challenge can be well-tackled if you have medical insurance, for instance. It allows you to take care of your bills, and you are easily treated without having to break your back to cater to the bills.

The other benefit of having insurance is that you do not get to start over after a misfortune. In a situation where you had a big business that encountered misfortune in the form of a fire or any accident that can sabotage the business, you can easily use your insurance cover the expenses and get out of the mess. As a businessman, you must not encounter a complete loss. The insurance helps you to pick up from the loss incurred and turn it into a successful outcome. Some losses can be difficult to recover from. Once they happen, it could mean that it is the end of a successful venture. At that point, you not only encounter a loss in terms of capital, but it also translates to an unachieved dream. To ensure that you do not get to this point in life, the insurance companies help you in avoiding complete losses. You might be wondering how you get insurance as a trader.

CHAPTER 2:

How to Start Day Trading

Day trading is becoming a lucrative engagement in the commerce industry with recent technological advancement. Hey there, welcome to the stock market world. This end is strategically oriented and plenty of fat risks coming your way. Let's dive into some of the factors that are likely to be considered.

The Capital Needed to Start Day Trading

Capital is so necessary to set the actual day trading ball on fire. Acquiring loans from different sites has been revealed to be so common among traders. With this glue on the mind, traders tend to be so careful with the amount of capital that they intend to commence with. To begin, traders are ought to obtain ready capital to monitor any kind of slight changes that are presumed to occur during the day.

Day trading requires a minimum account balance of $1000, but $8000-$ many providers and plenty of traders recommend 10,000 are not willing to risk 1% from the value. Also, the $1000 minimum amount that can be implemented can lead to your trading activities in being so not worthwhile.

Step by step kind of beginning is so vital because you get to acquire progress constantly and get to grow at a good speed with messing things out.

Let us look at some of the ways that are set to be considered:

Decide on what you will be trading.

Experts get their names by being good (perfect) in a particular field of trading. A stocks broker may be so bad in FOREX trading and vice versa. All the best in picking the best and the right one.

Sourcing for recommendations.

Sticking in mind that the actual amount of money to be used during trading is your own money, a wake-up call is assured and a good broker who can't be dodging with your precious money is super needed.

Try to even inquire from your colleagues you may have been in the previous spot or who they may have heard of good brokers. Try also to have some in-depth research from varieties of social media content, online reviews on the investment platforms, discussion boards and also take plenty of time to examine their websites.

Once you get several references, don't hesitate to check on their trading platforms. How were their actions? Any available complaints? How many traders have they ever been engaged with? How long have they been doing this? Have they been following the rules and regulations needed as a broker?

Commissions rate.

Even though the “perfect” broker is super needed as you begin day trading, consider in mind that this is also a new project as a whole. Meaning that profits too, need to be made so as this whole project can exist for a long while. Consider the rates of commissions that are likely to be spent to avoid any losses from being made. Pick an economical one to save yourself.

Executive Speed.

Any delay of seconds can result in a massacre to a trader’s profits. To prevent this, the broker should make sure that the trading activities are at a top-notch. The broker should be able to quickly spot any rapid changes that are likely to be incurred in the trading platforms.

Charting strategies.

Getting great chatting tools and software is also fundamental. Make sure you are getting good trading strategies, reliable variable markets, and better software features to enhance good day trading

Paper trading.

It’s advisable to begin day trading with paper trading, where you won’t have to use your own money, though many brokers highly discourage this. Know where your heart takes you.

Technology.

So, is the broker up for the new technological advancements? What kinds of accounts do they deal with? Does he/she have a real-time-data feed so that you can easily track and monitor trading activities? Which safeguard trading and Cybersecurity measures do they follow during trading? What kind of volumes of trading can they handle?

Greatly consider the kind who's so updated with the current technological happenings and pretty much informed.

Customer service provision.

Are they willing to offer customer service services? What happens when your system during mid-trade and it costs you so much? Are they going to support you to get much out of trading? Which process are they going to utilize during complaint resolution? And many more. Consider these before signing the contract because it's a big deal.

Safe, secure and regulated.

It's such a marvelous idea to inquire about the security of the broker in question. Inquire on how long they have been in business, their past work reports, what measures they have been using and their recent big measures on day trading. Make sure they regulated by an agency and that they strictly value and consider the rules and regulations needed to be followed by any broker engaged in day trading.

Adequate support.

Engage with brokers that are willing to provide huge support once there is a miss during your daily training activities. A few cents incremented on the broker's commission accounts is much worthwhile compared to hundreds of dollars losses that are likely to be incurred on the bad days.

How to Become a Day Trader

The following basic tools are recommended:

Computer/Monitor.

Well, cheap is expensive. A slow kind of computer can cause you a great fortune. Slow working implies that the day trading tracks to be unreliable and not trending. This is going to cost you in that the rates of profits at the end of any activity will be way low. They can cause you to miss trades, therefore, making your idea so unreliable. Remember you have a good reputation to uphold.

With all these in mind, please bear a quite fast laptop or monitor.

Set a target, really motivating.

Setting a realistic trading target is going to manage and monitor your real cash big time. A certain target is put for the purpose of big motivation. Work on that. Be for it big time. Remember achieving your target is normally tough because we all have really "dream" targets. Consistent losses will be incurred too, so prepare to lose some cash. Failure is never good though and will never be, so keep up champ!

Create a demo account.

Rehearsing has been always been a good move as your head to be successful navigation. Set up a demo account that will help you master all the ropes and moves that are likely to be incurred. Reading the fluctuations, the market trends are one way of future taking master moves that are great chances for high profitability rates. Keep testing and practicing until you are sure that you indeed set to go. Examine the market.

Master most of the trading moves. This makes you informed and enhances specialization in a particular field.

Fast internet connection.

A constant, fast and reliable type of internet connection is highly recommended. The unreliable internet connection can cause a miss in the market trends that can hinder the trading traces in a way leading to major losses being incurred at the end. Most of the users use a cable and ADSL type of connection. Remember that day trading does not recommend any unreliable source of connection.

Type of market.

Each kind of day trading demands a different kind of day trading. Choosing the kind of market to start with is super important, choose the most preferred.

Discover the tax implications likely to be incurred.

Inquire on how taxes revolve around profits. Engage with your financial adviser to let him or her explain how taxes are handled. Are they going to cause a devaluation on the made profits? Are they good news? How does that happen?

Be informed to at the end the trader can guess on the likelihood net profits to be expected.

Choose the right stocks to trade.

Well, to be better in choosing the right kind of stock, doing some in-depth research on the current existing stock is way the first step. Get to know the kind of stocks that are likely to perform well. Most preferably, those that are likely to perform well on a day-to-day basis. Remember to at least try one or two different kinds of stock until you are so sure that you have picked out the right one.

Plan a good financial figure.

You will need to prepare yourself early enough on the amount of money that can be risked on the day trading business. It is mostly advised not to risk more than 1-2% of your account money to avoid future losses.

Another piece of advice to the beginners, stay away from trading on the margin until you are set with enough moves and good trading wisdom. This will save you some extra cash in time.

Know the lingo.

Becoming an expert requires much effort. There are certain keywords that you are required to be familiar with. Check them out:

- Ask the amount of money a trader is offering for sale.
- Know the bid: This is the money amount a trader is ready to purchase.
- Stock breakouts: Declaring a stock that has experienced a breakout, basically talks of its reduction in the level of resistance.

- Candlestick: This is a type of chart specifically for prices that shows the maximum, minimum, opening and closing prices for a specified period.
- Covering: This refers to the buying back of the trade shares that had been sold earlier to do away with the obligation.
- Float: This is the amount of market share that is ready for day trading.
- Stock Gap Up or Down: This normally occurs when the price of a market trade becomes more or less than its previous closing price.
- The idea of Going Long: This normally refers to buying a market trade to offer it for sale at a higher price.
- High of Day and Low of Day: This is the highest or the lowest price a market trade has traded throughout the day.
- Hard to borrow list: This is ideally a list used by brokers that tells the stocks that are hard to borrow for short term sales.
- Market liquidity: This is a term that describes the state of the market showing how fast an inventory can be sold or purchased without affecting its price.
- Low Float Stock: This is a type of stock with a low amount of shares available for trading.

Market Maker: This term generally refers to any market participant, be it a firm or an individual who can purchase, sell and clear market trades. A market maker normally operates under given by-laws of a country.

CHAPTER 3:

How to Choose A Broker?

How to pick a broker for Options Trading?

Before opening an options trading account with a broker, how about we go over a couple of points to consider when we pick a broker.

- Understand your point when you track the options trading waters, regardless of whether it is a way of hedging risk, as a theoretical instrument, for income generation.
- Does the merchant or broker give option assessment devices of their own? It is always valuable to have access to an overabundance of apparatuses when you are choosing the right option.
- Enquire the commission charged by a broker and the transaction costs as this will eat into your investment profits.
- Some brokers offer access to inquire about materials in different areas of the stock market. You can generally check with the broker about access to investigate as well as subscription and so forth.

- Check the installment options given by the broker to ensure it is well-suited with your convenience.

Searching for the right broker

When the necessary background research is done, you can pick the right broker according to your need and comfort. In the worldwide market, a rundown of the top brokers is given underneath:

Rundown of Top International Brokers (Options Trading)

The rundown of top international options brokers is given underneath:

- E-trade ($0.65 per options contract)
- TD Ameritrade ($0.65 fee per contract)
- Ally Invest ($0.5 per contract traded)
- Schwab Brokerage ($0.65 per options contract)
- Interactive Brokers (starts at $0.25 per options contract)

List of Top Indian Brokers (Options Trading)

The list of top Indian Options Brokers is given below:

- ICICI Direct
- Axis Direct
- HDFC Securities
- ShareKhan

- Zerodha
- Kotak Securities
- Angel Broking

Amazing! Presently we take a look at certain options trading strategies that can be utilized in reality.

Tips for Picking an Option Broker

However, if you choose your options broker carefully, you'll quickly master how to coordinate research, track positions, and place trade.

Here's our proposal on picking a broker that offers the account features and the service that best serves your options trading requirements.

1. Search for a free education

In case you're new to options trading or need to extend your trading strategies, finding a dealer that has resources for educating clients is an absolute necessity. That training can come in numerous structures, including:

- Online options trading courses.
- Live or recorded online courses.
- One-on-one guidance by phone or online.
- A face-to-face meeting with a bigger dealer that has branches across the nation.

2. Put your broker's customer service to the test

Dependable customer service should be a high priority, especially for newer options traders. It's likewise significant for the individuals who are conducting complex trades or switching brokers they may need help with.

Consider what sort of contact you prefer. Email? Live online chat? Telephone support? Does the specialist/broker have a committed trading work area accessible if the need arises? What hours is it staffed? Is technical support available all day, every day, or just weekdays? Shouldn't something is said about delegates who can respond to inquiries regarding your account?

Even before you apply for an account, reach out and pose a few inquiries to check whether the appropriate responses and reaction time are palatable.

3. Make sure the trading platform is simple to utilize

Options trading platforms come in different shapes and sizes. They can be web-or programming based, work area or online just, have separate platforms for fundamental and propelled trading, offer full or incomplete mobile functionality or a combination of the abovementioned.

Visit a broker's site and search for a guided tour through its tools and platform. Video and screenshots instructional exercises are pleasant, but evaluating a dealer's simulated trading platform, f it has one, will give you the best feeling of whether the broker is a solid match.

A few interesting points:

- Is the platform structure easy to use or do you need to hunt and peck to discover what you need?
- How simple is it to place a trade?
- Can the platform do the things you need, such as making alerts dependent on explicit models or letting you fill out an exchange ticket advance to submit later?
- Will you need mobile access to the full set-up of service when you are on the go, or will a pared-down rendition of the platform do the trick?
- How solid is the site, and how rapidly are orders executed? This is a high priority if your strategy includes rapidly entering and leaving positions.
- Does the broker charge a month to month or yearly platform fee? Assuming this is the case, are there approaches to get the expense waived, for example, conducting a certain number of trades or keeping a minimum account balance during a particular period?
- Evaluate the depth, breadth, and cost of tools and data

Research and Data are an options broker's backbone. Some of the nuts and bolts to search for:

- Frequently updated statements feed.
- Basic diagramming to help pick your exit and entry points
- The ability to dissect a trade's potential rewards and risks (maximum downside and maximum upside).
- Screening devices.

Those wandering into further developed trading strategies may require further expository and trade modeling instruments, for example, customizable screeners; the ability to construct, test, track and back-test trading techniques; and real-time market information from numerous providers.

Verify whether the fancy stuff costs more. For instance, most brokers give free deferred quotes, lagging twenty minutes behind market information, however, charge an expense for an ongoing feed. Likewise, some master level instruments might be available just to clients who meet month to month or account balance or quarterly trading activity.

5. Do not weigh the cost of commissions too heavily

There is a reason commission costs are lower on our rundown. Price isn't all that matters, and it's not as significant as other things we've covered. However, since commissions give a suitable side by side correlation, they often are the main things people see when choosing an options broker.

A couple of things to think about how much brokers charge to trade options:

- The two segments of an options trading commission are the base rate — basically equivalent to the thing as the trading commission that financial specialists pay when they purchase a stock — and the per-contract fee. Commissions have been reduced recently; various brokers directly offer free commissions. Contract costs are between 15 cents to 1.25USD or more.
- Some brokers pack the trading commission and the per-contract expense into a solitary flat charge.
- Some brokers additionally offer limited commissions dependent on trading recurrence, average, or volume account balance. The meaning of "active trader" or "high volume" varies by the brokerage.

In case you're new to options trading or utilize the strategy just sparingly you will well-served by picking either a specialist that offers a solitary level rate to exchange or one that charges no commission (you likely won't have the option to avoid the per-contract expense). In case you're a more active dealer, you should audit your trading rhythm to check whether a layered pricing plan would save you cash.

Choosing an Online Options Broker

Of the considerable number of choices, you make before really beginning to trade options, the decision of which online options specialist to utilize is without a doubt one of the more significant ones. Such a choice isn't irreversible because you can generally utilize an alternate specialist if the first you try does not exactly work out for you. However, it merits investing energy choosing which one to sign up within the beginning.

Utilizing the right agent truly can positively affect your trading. Online dealers are continually improving and they generally make the entire procedure for purchasing and selling options substantially more effective and simple to do. That is just obvious, however, if you utilize one of the top brokers that are truly good at giving a five-star service.

The procedure for picking a broker is not hard, however, there is a ton to consider. There are such huge numbers of decisions out there. Although they all offer a similar sort of service, some of them may be more reasonable for you than others. Not every trader is going to have exactly the very same prerequisites which makes it extremely hard to say that a particular dealer is "the best." What may be directly for one broker may not be right for another.

The key is truly to work out what is essential to you and afterward do some examination to discover which specialist is probably going to be the most useful for your very own needs. We have a segment devoted to the Best Options Brokers that you may like to investigate, however, we would propose that you originally read through this page where we have covered a portion of the primary factors that you ought to consider.

- Quality and Speed of Order Execution
- Commissions and Fees
- Security Measures
- Trading Platform and Ease of Use
- Reputation
- Additional Considerations
- Customer Support

Commissions and Fees

It's to some level logical that one of the most significant contemplations while picking an online dealer or broker is what that the charges are. Charges can essentially be separated into two primary classifications: commissions and other fees.

Commissions are charged on each exchange that you make, whether you are purchasing or selling options, thus it can mean a sizable sum if you are making a lot of transactions. A few brokers likewise have a base commission and this is something to pay special mind to if you are planning to make various little exchanges; some may charge higher commissions relying upon what sort of option is being transacted.

The extra fees can envelop an entire scope of various charges including a yearly charge just for having an account, charges for withdrawals and deposits, or additional expenses for making particular sorts of orders.

Contingent upon what strategies and trading styles you are utilizing, you might be making exchanges that will just generate profits that are moderately little contrasted with the sum contributed. It isn't at all remarkable for options traders to work on very tight edges, and this makes it critical to decrease the costs associated with making trades.

Hence, before you sign up at a broker you ought to know about their commission structure and any extra expenses that can be applied so you can be certain that their charges are reasonable for how you will be trading. However, it's likewise important that commissions and charges are not the ends of it. They are significant, however somewhat the facts confirm that you get what you pay for. The least expensive brokers are not the best, and it tends to merit paying somewhat more if you feel a more costly broker is better for you in other zones.

One specific reason behind paying more would be if you needed some assistance while you were beginning. Most online dealers are known as discount agents since they keep their commissions low and their service is essentially just to transact the orders that you tell them to. There are also full-service merchants, which regularly charge at a higher rate, yet give you the advantage of an experienced proficient on hand to offer you guidance and advice.

CHAPTER 4:

What Is the Best Market for Day Trading?

You need to know your way around the options market to leverage your daily investments. Many day traders begin with the stock market simply because there are many similar nuances between options and stocks. Trading stocks is what most people immediately think of when they hear day trading. Therefore, it is in every options day trader to become familiar with the stock market as well even though the trader should never confuse the two entities.

Deciding What Market to Trade In

Before you jump into the market looking for options to trade, you need to decide what type of assets are good for day trading options. Not doing so will only leave you feeling dazed and confused because the market can seem endless. Yes, stocks are the easy, popular choice but they are not the only choice and they might not be the right choice for you. Futures, forex, cryptocurrencies and even corn are also good options for day trading options. Stock trading is facilitated by the buying and selling of shares in a company's portfolio and day trading stock options means that all positions must be opened by 9:30 AM EST and closed by 4 PM EST on the American stock market.

The future market is one where the contract is created between the seller and the trader to buy or sell a predetermined value of the associated asset at a future date. An options day trader can profit due to the price fluctuations that can happen in the space of a day. The day trader needs to be cautious with the futures market working hours because they can vary. As such, the trader needs to be aware of the time his or her position needs to close.

The forex market is accessible at any time of day and is the biggest financial market in the world. This market allows for the exchange of different currencies.

There are many more markets to choose from when starting your options day trading career. Still, it all boils down to your circumstances and the resources you have available to you. For example, startup fund can be an issue. This is particularly prevalent with the stock market. On the stock market, a trader needs to have an excess of $20,000 on his or her trading account to participate. In contrast, the forex market allows trades that are as low as a few hundred dollars. Therefore, you can only pursue options in the stock and futures market if you have the capital to back you.

Time is another consideration. Remember that some markets like the stock market only function at certain times of day, some fluctuate in time operation and others operate 24 hours a day.

Strategy is also a factor., but some strategies work best in certain market at certain times of day. Therefore, if there is a particular strategy that a day trader is great at then he or she might have better results in certain markets.

How to Find the Best Options to Day Trade

After you have set your sights on a particular market, then you can move on to determine which particular assets you will pursue options in. You need to be able to pinpoint niches that work and luckily there are systems in place that can help you do that. Such tools include:

Technical Analysis

This is the first tool that we will discuss. It allows day traders to examine market sectors to identify strengths and weaknesses. By identifying those strengths and weakness, the options day trader can narrow down the options niches he or she would like to pursue within a given market.

There are several types of tools for performing technical analysis and they include:

- Bollinger Band, which is a measure of market volatility.
- Intraday momentum index (IMI), which is an indicator of how options will play out within 1 day.
- Open Interest (OI), which indicates the number of open options contracts to determine trends in options.
- Money Flow Index (MFI), which indicates the flow of money into assets over specific amount of times.

- Relative Strength Index (RSI), which allows the trader to compare profits and losses over a set period.
- Put-Call Ratio (PCR), which indicates the volume of the put options relative to call options.

Price Charts

These tools gives visual representation of price and volume information so that market trends can be determined. More precisely known as price charts because they show price movement over a specific amount of time, charts come in different types. Common types include:

Line Charts

These easy-to-interpret charts document price movement over a specific period such as months or years. Each price data point is connected using a single line.

While the biggest advantage this type of chart is the simplicity, this also causes a disadvantage to day traders as they provide no information about the strength of trading during the day.

The line chart also does not provide price gap information. A price gap is defined as the interval between one trading periods that is completely above or below a previous trading period.

This price cap information is critical for options day traders to have to make effective decisions.

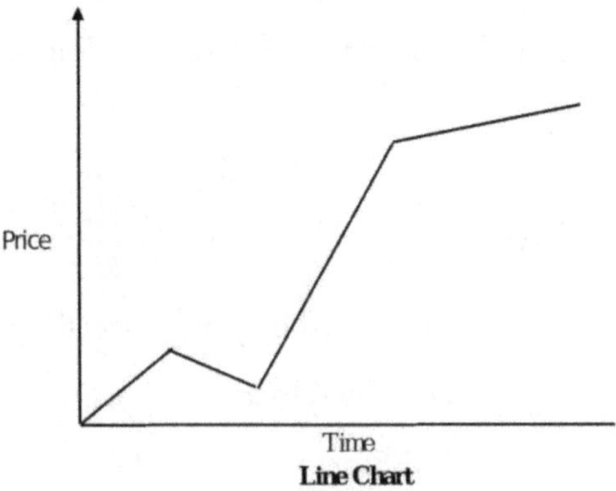

Line Chart

Open-High-Low-Close Bar Chart

This type of chart illustrates price movement from highest to lowest over as specific amount of time such as 1 hour or one day. It is so named because it shows open, high, low and close prices for the period specified. The low to high trading range is displayed with a vertical line. In contrast, the opening and closing prices are displayed on a horizontal tab. All four elements make up one bar on the chart and a series of these bars show movement over an extended period.

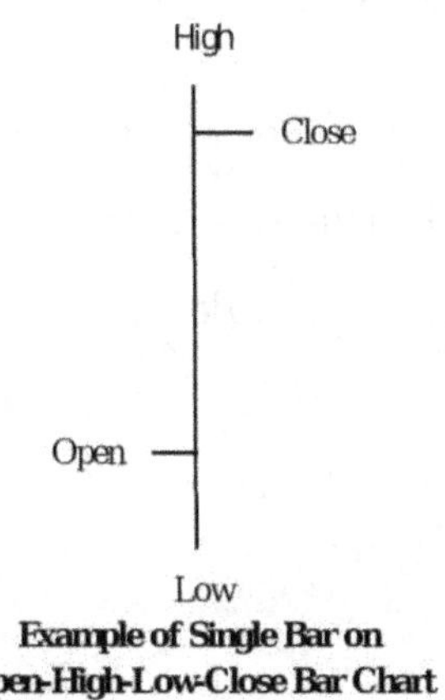

Example of Single Bar on Open-High-Low-Close Bar Chart

This type of bar chart is advantageous as an options day trading tool because it provides information over 1-day trading periods as well as price gap knowledge.

Candlestick Chart

This is the kind of chart that is used by professional options day traders. It is similar to the open-high-low-close bar chart and is represented by price on the vertical axis and time on horizontal axis.

As such, it depicts price movement over time.

The structure of the candlestick chart has individual components.

They are called candlesticks, hence the name of the chart.

Every candlestick has 3 parts.

They are called:

- The body. This depicts the open-to-close range.
- The wick. This represents the daily highs and lows. It is also called the shadow.
- The color. This depicts the direction of price movement. White or green indicate an upward price movement. Red or black indicate a price decline.

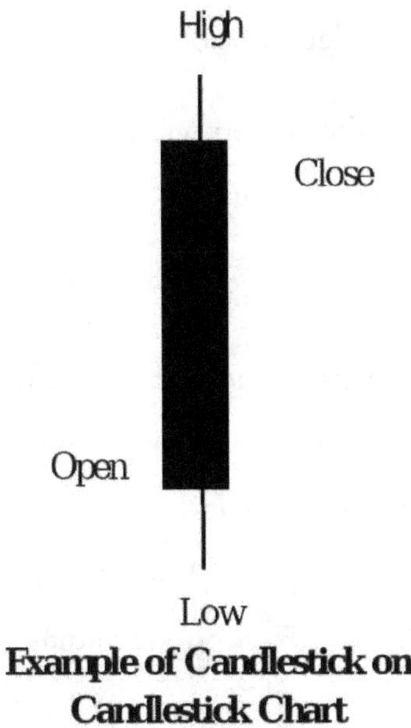

Example of Candlestick on Candlestick Chart

Using the candlestick chart allows day traders to see patterns on the market. There are several types of candlestick charts.

Factors that Affect the Options Market

After you have analyzed the options market and decided on the options that you will pursue, it is time to navigate the market and make a bet on the options you have decided on.

The first thing you need to do is execute a trade. If you are using an online broker as most options day traders do these days, you will make an order through the broker's digital system. When this is done, the options day trader needs to identify whether or not, he or she will be opening a new position or closing an existing position.

After this has successfully been executed, the trade details will be sent to the options day trader electronically.

Factors that affect how the option will play out include interest rates, economic trends and market volatility.

Chapter Summary

An options day trader needs to know his or her way around the options market to be effective at this career. The first thing the day trader needs to do is decide on the particular market that he or she will trade options in. The stock market is a popular choice but it requires a high initial investment and has set hours for options trading.

The futures and forex market are also popular options trading markets with different operating times and lower initial investment amount requirements. These might work better for some options day traders.

After the options day trader has figured out the particular market that he or she will trade options in, he or she has to pick a particular niche within that market to trade options in. Using technical analysis and price charts like the line chart, open-high-low-close bar chart and candlestick chart help options day traders decide on the best options to pursue.

After this decision has been made, the day trader will execute the options trade via the brokerage firm he or she works with. This is typically done online as most options day traders turn to digital means in this age of technology. The success of how this options trade will play out is affected by factors like interest rates, economic trends and market volatility.

CHAPTER 5:

Buying Long and Selling Short

Regardless of the way of stock, some will bring in cash when the value changes and others lose. The clarification for this is the divergence between the long purchase and short sell. On the off chance that it comes to securities exchange exchanging, you start an exchange by purchasing first or selling first, the words long and short apply to buy to sell at a more significant expense, later on, you may begin a long exchange and make a benefit. You may likewise execute a short deal by selling the stock at a lower cost and making a benefit before buying.

What's a Short Sell?

Let me offer a nitty gritty depiction. Short selling is a contributing or exchanging work on hypothesizing on the fall in the cost of a stock or different protections. Dealers may utilize a short deal as influence, and financial specialists or reserve supervisors can utilize it as a fence against the drawback danger of a prolonged situation in the equivalent or comparative assurance. Hypothesis brings critical hazard prospects and is an inventive type of trade. Supporting is an increasingly regular exchange including the situation of a balancing position to diminish hazard.

A position is opened in short selling by getting portions of a stock, or different resources that the bank accept will diminish in an incentive by a predefined future date—the expiry date. At that point the loan specialist offers those obtained offers to financial specialists who can follow through available cost. The broker is wagering that the cost will keep on falling until you return the obtained stock with the goal that they can get them at a lower rate. The possibility of misfortune on a short deal is conceivably constant, as each benefit's cost could ascend to endlessness.

How Short Selling Works

The vender opens a situation in short selling by acquiring shares, for the most part from an agent vendor. They'll attempt to profit by utilizing those offers before returning them to the moneylender.

A broker must have an edge record to open a short position, and would regularly need to pay enthusiasm on the estimation of the obtained shares while the position is open. Additionally, the Financial Industry Regulatory Authority, Inc. (FINRA), authorizes the principles and guidelines managing authorized specialists and intermediary seller firms in the United States. The New York Stock Exchange (NYSE), and the Federal Reserve have set least sums for the sum to be held by the edge account—known as the support edges. On the off chance that the record estimation of a financial specialist falls beneath the support edge, you will require more assets, or the intermediary will sell the position.

A financial specialist repurchases the offers available—ideally at a cost not as much as what they acquired the benefit — to close a little benefit, and returns them to the moneylender or dealer. Merchants are required to represent any intrigue paid on exchanges by the intermediary or commissions.

The merchant deals with the errand of finding borrowable protections and returning them off camera toward the finish of the exchange. Like most specialists, you can make the exchange open and close through the standard exchanging stages. Through representative does, in any case, have necessities that the exchanging account must meet previously taking into account edge exchanging. As referenced before, hypothesis is one of the essential explanations behind engaging in short selling.

Short Selling for a Profit

Picture a dealer who accept that in the following three months, XYZ stock — as of now exchanging at $50—will fall in cost. They obtain and offer the 100 offers to another financial specialist. The broker is presently 100 "delicate" shares as they sold something they didn't claim however acquired from. Acquiring the offers permitted the short selling, which may not generally be conceivable if different brokers as of now abbreviate the stock gradually.

After seven days, the enterprise whose offers were abbreviated reports the quarter's poor money related execution, and the stock is down to $40. The broker needs to close the short position and purchases on the open market 100 offers for $40 to supplant the obtained stock. The advantage for the broker on the short deal, less commissions, and edge account intrigue is $1,000.

Short selling for a misfortune

Utilizing the above model, how about we presently state the dealer didn't close the short situation at $40 yet chose to leave it open to benefit from a further fall in costs. Regardless, an adversary plunges in with a takeover offer of $65 an offer to purchase the organization, and the stock takes off. On the off chance that the dealer chooses to close the short situation at $65, the short sell misfortune would be $1,500: ($50-$ 65= negative $15x 100 shares= loss of $1,500). There, to cover their position, the dealer needed to repurchase the stock at an altogether more significant expense.

Short selling as a fence

Notwithstanding theory, a short deal has another valuable reason— supporting — frequently saw as the lower hazard and progressively decent short-selling model. The primary role of supporting is barrier, rather than the theory's unadulterated benefit inspiration. Supporting is done to make sure about benefits or diminish misfortunes in a portfolio. In any case, as it comes at an impressive cost, by far most of retail speculators don't think about it during ordinary occasions.

The expense of supporting is twofold. There's the immediate expense of putting on the support, incorporating the expenses related with short deals, or the premiums accused for agreements of security alternatives. Regardless of whether stocks will in general ascent higher, there's the open door danger of topping the portfolio upside. Short selling advantages and disadvantages can be expensive if the merchant misestimates the value change. A broker who has bought stock will lose only 100 percent of their cost if the stock tumbles to zero.

A broker who has shorted stock, be that as it may, can lose substantially more than 100 percent of their unique speculation. The risk originates from the absence of a breaking point at the cost of a stock; it might develop to boundlessness and past — to acquire a term from another comic character, Buzz Light-year. Likewise, the broker needed to subsidize the edge account while holding the stocks. Additionally, if everything is going great while assessing their income, brokers will factor in the cost of the edge esteem.

Pros

✓ Possibility of high benefits

✓ No underlying capital required

✓ Proportionate ventures conceivable

✓ Hedge against different resources

Cons

✓ Potentially boundless misfortunes

✓ Potential boundless edge of intrigue acquired

✓ Short presses

With regards to bringing a deal to a close, a short-dealer may experience difficulty discovering enough offers to buy—alternately, if the market, or a particular stock, begins soaring, venders can be caught in a short crush circle.

Then again, high-hazard approaches offer a high return reward as well. Short deals are no exemption. In the event that the vender accurately gauges the value moves, they will make a clean rate of profitability (ROI), basically in the event that they use edge to begin the deal.

Having edge offers influence, guaranteeing that the dealer didn't need to provide a lot of their cash as an underlying venture. Short selling can be a compelling method to support, furnishing other portfolio protections with an offset, whenever finished with care.

Notwithstanding the hazard above of losing cash on an exchange from the value ascent of a stock, short selling represents extra dangers that financial specialists should think about.

Obtained cash shortening is known as edge exchanging. You open an edge account when short selling, which permits you to obtain cash from the business firm utilizing your venture as insurance.

Much the same as when you're on a huge edge, misfortunes are anything but difficult to turn crazy since you need to satisfy the 25 percent least upkeep prerequisite. You will be dependent upon an edge call if your record falls beneath this, and you will be compelled to place in more money or sell your position.

Wrong planning

Albeit an organization is exaggerated, the stock cost will perhaps require a significant stretch of time to fall. While, you're powerless against intrigue, edge calls, and summoning.

The Short Squeeze

In the event that a stock with a high short buoy and days to cover proportion is brisk, it is likewise in danger of encountering a short press. In the event that a stock keeps on growing, a short crush happens, and short-merchants spread their wagers by repurchasing their short positions. This buy will turn into an input circle. Offer interest draws in more speculators, driving the stock higher, provoking a lot progressively short-venders to repurchase or spread their positions.

Administrative dangers

To maintain a strategic distance from disarray and unjustifiable selling pressure, controllers can here and there place bans on short deals in a specific segment or even in the expansive market. These practices can cause an abrupt spike in stock costs, compelling short dealers to cover short situations at colossal misfortunes.

Moving Against Trend

Proof has demonstrated stocks have an upward pattern when all is said in done. The heft of stocks ascend in cost over the long haul. So far as that is concerned, regardless of whether a firm is scarcely improving throughout the years, the economy's expansion or value rise rate will push its stock cost up to some degree. This means brevity wagers against the general market course.

Short selling costs

In contrast with purchasing and holding stocks or offers, short selling includes significant expenses, notwithstanding the typical exchanging charges that agents need to pay. Any of the costs incorporate Net Interest Market premium can be a critical cost when exchanging net stocks. Since short deals must be made through edge accounts, the intrigue payable on short exchanges may include after some time, mainly if short positions are kept open over an all-encompassing period.

Profits and different Fees

The short dealer is answerable for making profit installments to the organization from which the stock was acquired on the shorted stock. The short merchant is additionally on the snare for making installments because of other shorted stock-related occurrences, including share parts, side projects, and reward share issues, the two of which are capricious episodes.

Short Selling Metrics

Two measurements used to follow the short-selling movement on a stock are Short Interest Ratio (SIR) known as the Short Float measures the offer proportion at present

CHAPTER 6:

The Main Strategies of Day Trading

The truth is that many people tend to use investing as a side hustle. However, the truth is that you can do amazing things by merely trading for a living. So, in this part, we will help you to understand and create a plan. Where you can eventually make options trading, your business and start making a full-time income with it. One thing to keep in mind, depending on where you live the tips and tricks provided to you may be different. Therefore, it is advised that you look at your countries laws before you make any changes.

If you are only planning to do options trading as a hobby, you can buy small numbers of options and try to profit on them and see what happens. Most people hope to build up their options trading activities, eventually turning it into a business so that they can earn a living from it and drop the "9 to 5." In this part, we provide some tips and advice for turning your options trading activities into a business that makes real money. Start Small, the first thing to do is to learn the way of the industry. Having smaller ambitions that can be realized is going to be a part of laying a successful foundation for an options trading business. Many new traders want to get going fast and so purchase lots of options simultaneously, and if they can get higher approval levels, enter into multiple strategies all at once. The reality is that options trading are complicated and a lot more complicated than buying and selling stocks, and so you should keep things under control rather than jumping in and getting in a situation where your mind cannot possibly fully comprehend, analyze, and keep track of a dozen complicated options trades. Begin by limiting yourself to five companies and index funds to use in your trading.

In fact, during the first three months, you might limit yourself to 2-3 companies. You should study the stock of those companies and learn its fundamentals, studying the stock charts to see how the stock has moved in the past. Learn essential facts about the companies such as when they are going to have their following earnings call. You should also learn some basics about spotting and tracking trends in the markets. This can include learning how to read candles, using moving averages, and spotting levels of support and resistance, which can tell you when to enter a trade and when to get out of a trade. Starting small also means setting small goals and meeting them, rather than hoping to make $10,000 a month in profits right away. So, plan on entering trades to make a hundred or a few hundred dollars a week and realize that you are not going to win at every trade. As you gain experience, you can increase the sizes of your trades. But rather than entering ten different trades, you should always aim to do multiples of the same options contracts instead, so you don't run into the problem of having too much to manage at once. Remember that options have an expiration date and change fast, so keeping close track of them is essential.

Adequate Capital You can trade options for as little as less than $100, but it is not likely that you are going to be able to build a full-time income that way. You should plan on setting up an account with $5,000 or more in Capital to get started. If you don't have access to that much money now, you can start trading 1-2 options per week using small amounts of money to start learning and trying out different strategies. But plan on having a minimum of $5,000 when you transition to doing options trading as a business and plan on growing the size of your account with time. Uses a Broker with Complete Resources We've mentioned Robinhood, and it's an excellent platform for beginners. If you've never traded options before, we recommend that you open a Robinhood account and spend 2-3 months trading on Robinhood to gain some experience. However, when you are ready to transition trading as a business, a more comprehensive platform is going to be necessary. One thing you'll want to make sure of is that you can sell options naked. That isn't possible on Robinhood.

You should also seek out a broker that has comprehensive resources that can be used to do all of your research, analyze your trades, and execute the trades all in one platform. As an options trader, you're going to be wanting to track your options, but also keeping a close eye on the stock itself and even on the news about the company. At the very least, you should be able to view the stock and your options simultaneously comfortably. Depending on your brokerage, you may be able to set things up so that you can see everything associated with one stock ticker with a click. Make a Business Plan You wouldn't open a restaurant without making a business plan, and if you are going to have a trading business, you should treat it the same way. Write out a business plan that outlines goals, expenses, and other items so that you have everything laid out, including Capital that will be available for funding.

Only starting to buy and sell options and seeing what happens is not a business, although it can be a start. Also, keep track of all your trades, so you can carefully monitor profit and loss. Part of your business plan will be setting goals for annual returns. Possible returns on options are quite high compared to stocks, but you should set realistic goals to ensure you're staying grounded and meeting them. Also, remember that you have to take losses into account and not just to look at wins to determine your total return on investment. Decide on a Business Structure Are you going to set up a business to run your trades? It's worth doing so.

Otherwise, you will have a hard time deducting loss from your taxes. The IRS views trading as ordinary passive income, and there are limits to what you can deduct. You can try to get the "trader" status, but this is difficult. The easiest way to set things up so that you can fully deduct losses and expenses, and possibly offer yourself bankruptcy protection if it came to that, is to set up an official business entity that you can use to trade through. You will not be doing this as a sole proprietor but will instead need to set up an LLC or S-Corporation. An LLC is simpler to set up and acts as a pass-through, but you will be able to manage your expenses deduct everything as a professional trader and then pass on the profits as income to your personal life. The details of this are beyond the scope of this hardback, so speak to an accountant about setting this up if necessary. Note those individuals who want to be treated as professional traders by the IRS have to be qualified; an LLC set up for trading purposes does not. It's complicated to be treated by the IRS as a fulltime trader as an individual, and you have to derive the majority of your income from trading to qualify. It turns out that even people who derive their full-time income from trading have trouble qualifying, and when you don't qualify, you're going to have a hard time deducting all of your expenses and losses. So, starting an LLC and having it to the trading and then pass the profits onto you as the owner is probably the best way to get started trading. Stay Focused It is better to stay focused on one type of trading, learn it thoroughly, and commit to it 100%. Don't be all over the map, such as trying to trade Forex or Crypto and options at the same time. If you are going to try options trading, then stick to options trading. Be serious about if you want success to the level of having it provide a full-time income.

Are You Going to Utilize Debt this is a personal decision, but it's not recommended that you utilize debt unless there is some compelling reason that you start with an account with a particular size? The ease of doing small options trades and earning profits means that most people are better off starting small and then reinvesting profits to increase the size of their trades going forward. If you take out loans to get started, keep the loan size reasonable, and don't get more loans if you have a string of losses, you don't want to dig a hole you can't get out of. Set a reasonable maximum for borrowed Capital such as $5,000-$10,000. Set a Time Limit If a year goes by and you are continually losing money, you will have to evaluate whether or not options trading is for you. The reality is it's not for everyone. That doesn't mean that stocks or trading full-time aren't in your future, but if it is not working out after putting in significant effort, you should re-evaluate your position and consider alternatives. For example, maybe you would be better suited to work as a swing or day trader or get into Forex, rather than trading options. Constantly Educate Yourself. You should be continually improving your knowledge of the field. That means educating yourself by reading profit and loss on options trading, watching YouTube videos, taking Udemy courses, and possibly taking more expensive courses. You wouldn't try becoming an engineer, doctor, or lawyer without getting the education first, so treat trading the same way if you are expecting to earn a full-time income from it.

CHAPTER 7:

Types of Chart

Technical analysts use a different method to analyze the price patterns in markets. The techniques used include:

Chart Patterns

These are patterns where the prices are drawn on charts inform of graphs. When data is drawn on the graph, there is always a repetitive pattern. This pattern shows the movement of the prices in the forex markets. It shows the strength and the weakness of the trade. Some forex traders use the chart patterns as continuation signals or the reversal signals.

The continuous signals contain, triangle, flag and pennant, channel and cup with the handle while the reversal includes, double top reversal, double bottom reversal, triple top reversal, head and shoulders and so many other. There are three groups of chart patterns that traders use — these chart patterns area the candlestick patterns, the harmonic patterns, and the traditional patterns.

The technical analysts using this chart patterns use horizontal lines, trend lines, and the Fibonacci retracement level to find the signals of the chart patterns. The chart patterns show the strengths and weaknesses of the forex market.

Fibonacci Levels

These levels in chart patterns exhume the hidden support and resistance. The support and resistance can be hidden due to the golden ratios. The origin pf Fibonacci is from the mathematical proportion, but it acts like the old support and resistance in the chart patterns when the price levels are laid out. The mathematical proportions used in this method is very different from the highs and the lows on the price charts.

Candlestick Patterns

Forex technical analysts use to find the open, high, and low-price levels in the markets (OHL). The prices sought must be of a specific period in the trading session so that a comparison of the trader's behavior during the trade is made against the prices at that particular time. This analysis will help in predicting the future price movement in the forex trade market.

Horizontal Lines

These lines are also called sideways trends. These lines connect the lows and the highs in the variables. In this case the prices on the charts. These lines show the price that is below the support level and above the resistance level.

Trend lines

Trend lines are lines drawn on the chart or the graph to show support or resistance. These trend lines are dependent on the direction in which the prices are going in the forex trade. They are also known as horizontal support and resistance. When analysts are using trend lines in the chart patterns, they can see the increase or decrease in supply and demand.

The traders make up their mind whether to invest or not when this increase or decrease occur. When the prices are going up, it is called an upward trend, and the forex traders can sell. When the prices are going down, it is called a downward trend, and buyers can make their entry in the trade.

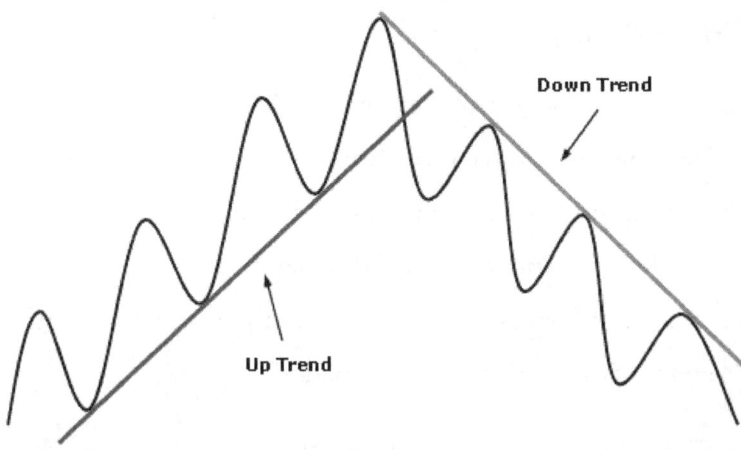

Technical Analysis Indicators

The technical forex analysts use the price action indicator. These indicators include;

The moving average

The moving average indicator shows the averages of prices in a given period. The moving averages display the direction of the market. The moving average helps balance the prices in the market by removing the unwanted prices. This removal helps the trader focus on the trend of the prices in the market. There are four types of the moving averages, namely the exponential moving averages (EMA), simple moving averages (SMA), linear weighted average (LWA), and the smoothed averages.

Bollinger Bands

This indicator is a tool used in technical analysis that comprises of three lines. These lines are plotted positively and negatively but away from the simple moving average of the currency price. These lines are adjustable to the trader's preference. The Bollinger bands help measure the variation degree of prices during the trade. In simpler terms, it measures the volatility of the market in a given period.

Amongst the three lines in the Bollinger, the middle line shows the trend direction of the prices while the upper and lower lines are the volatility lines, also called the volatility bands. The upper and the lower bands are moved above and below the middle band by two standard deviations. This movement of the upper and the lower bands put the price between the two outside lines. This price does not stay here for a long time because it is always moving around the middle line.

Gives an Early signal

The technical signal traders and investors early on when the time is right to invest. It is like a wake-up call to go in or come in or out of the trade. The correct entry or exit time for traders will help them good gains on their trades.

Support and resistance

Know support and resistance is crucial to achieving the success you are looking for when it comes to technical analysis and while they may seem complex at first, they will become clearer every time you put the theory around them into practice. At their most basic, resistance can be thought of as the ceiling on the price of a particular currency or currency pair which means the price is unlikely to move past this point while support can be thought of as the price floor where it is unlikely to decrease any further.

The concept of support and resistance is actually quite simple: if a stock touches support, similar to a floor, it may be a good time to buy (because the price is likely to rise). And when a stock hits resistance, similar to a ceiling, selling may be a good time (because the price is likely to fall). Think of support and resistance as a trade zone, not exact price levels.

To be even more specific, support is the price at which the price of a stock has stopped falling and either moved sideways (e.g., the price is moving horizontally) or reversed.

At this level, selling pressure dropped, and stock demand was strong enough to keep the price from falling further. Demand will exceed supply and prevent falling prices.

Resistance, on the other hand, is the price at which selling pressure is strong enough to prevent stock from further rising. Supply exceeds demand, purchasing pressure has stopped. More sellers will enter the market, preventing higher stocks.

Technicians analyze charts to determine what happens when a stock reaches key support or resistance. Often, a stock's price will reverse and bounce off support or resistance. Many day-traders act when a stock breaks through support or resistance.

Charts and Indicators

Trend lines, Level Lines and Channels

Perhaps the most important portion of your charting time will be spent on drawing (which is also known as plotting) trend lines, horizontal lines and parallel channel lines. As you can see, (B) displays these three types of lines. As a novice trader, I found it very interesting to learn that the market moves in certain directions following a simple trend line or respecting a certain horizontal level line.

The Moving Average Convergence Divergence (MACD)

This price indicator shows the momentum of the market. It shows when the market is doing well or not and the force behind this action. While using this indicator, a signal will always be evident is a market is moving in one direction. The Moving Average Convergence Divergence indicator belongs to a class of oscillators. Oscillators are technical indicators too and shown separately, below the prices in the charts.

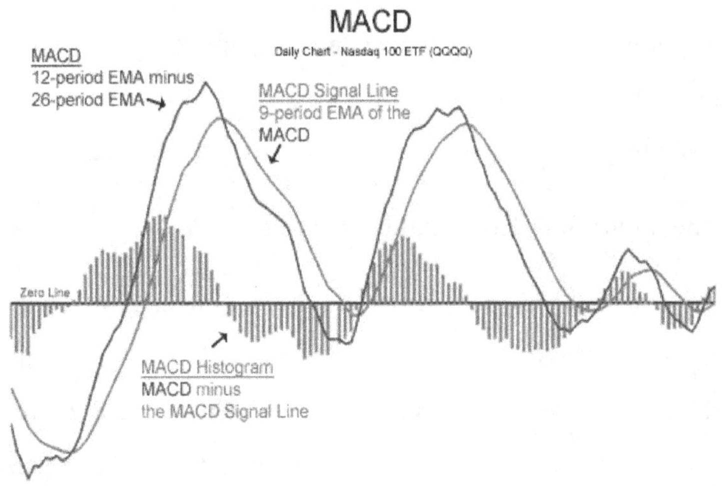

Principle of Technical analysis

Price Moves according to trends

Technical analyses assume that the prices in the trend move according to the trend patterns. The prices move in a bullish trend, bearish trend, and the sideways trend.

All price movements repeat themselves

The theory in this principle called the Dow Theory assumes that the price of a commodity represents its actual value, and it does not have to look at other factors. The principle claim that the prices in the patterns are repetitive and any future price is likely to be the same as the current price.

Advantages of Technical Analysis

Shows the Trend of the Market

Technical analysis shows the traders direction of the market. They can know the time the downward movement of prices and the upward movement, hence enabling them to make to sell or buy at the appropriate time.

Shows the trader Both Entry and Exit points

Timing is essential to a person trading in the forex. Poor timing will cause significant losses, and which will cause the trade to fail. The technical analysis predicts the time for investment for traders. It gives traders the upper hand to know when entering the trade or exit that trade.

Different indicators in technical analysis aids traders get the advantage of knowing investment time early. The candlesticks, moving averages, chart patterns, trend lines, and other indicators help in the calculation of the entry and the exit time in the trade.

Technical Analysis is fast

Technical analysis is fast in giving information about a specific trade. This action makes it quick and reliable to short term traders like the intraday traders who trade in one minute to thirty minutes. In this trade, candlestick patterns are used.

Technical Analysis Gives Adequate Information

Short term traders use technical analysis, swing traders, and long-term traders. Enough information is found in the chart patterns, and forex traders can use this information to their advantage. The traders can pursue their trades utilizing this information and get satisfying returns. More details like the trading psychology, market momentum, volatility, support, and resistance are a portion of the vital information that the technical analysis provides.

Technical Analysis is Cheap

Technical analysis of soft wares is cheap. Some soft wares are free offers from different charting software companies, and they can even be downloaded on mobile apps.

CHAPTER 8:

Candlesticks

The Japanese began using technical analysis to trade rice in the 1600s. This early version is different than what the US used that was introduced by Charles Dow about 1900 though the principles are similar:

- The action of the price is above everything else like earnings, news, etc.
- All information is reflected in price.
- Sellers and buyers keep the market moving based on greed and fear.
- Markets will fluctuate.
- There's a possibility that prices won't show underlying value.

Candlestick charting appeared around 1850. The credit for developing candlestick charting goes to a rice trader Homma who lived in Sakata. His ideas were probably refined and modified from many years of trading and eventually, the results were the charts we use now.

To make a candlestick chart, you will need data for the close, low, high, and open values for the times that you need to have displayed. The portion that is hollow or filled is called the body. The thin lines that are above or below show the high or low range. They are called shadows. These are called tails or wicks, too. The high gets shown by peak of the top shadow and you see the low with lower shadow. When, a hollow candlestick is drawn at the bottom indicating the opening price and the top indicating the closing. When it's lower than opening, the candlestick is colored in at the top indicating the opening price and the bottom indicating the closing.

When it gets compared to normal bar charts, most traders think that candlestick charts are easier to read and look better. Each candlestick will show a way to figure out the price action. The trader is able to look at the relationship of open and close and the highs and lows. These relationships are vital information that proves how significant candlesticks are. Hollow ones will show buying pressure. This is when the closing is bigger than the opening. Filled candlesticks will show selling pressure. This shows the closing was less than the opening.

The longer the body, the greater the selling or buying pressure. Short ones show that consolidation and price movements were low.

Strong buying pressure is shown by long white candlesticks. A longer candlestick, the farther the closing was above the opening. This will show that the price grew more from opening to closing and buyers were aggressive. Long white candlesticks are bullish. There is a lot that goes into their big picture. Once a decline happens, a turning point will be seen with a long white candlestick.

Long black candlesticks indicate there is a lot of selling pressure. The length of the candlestick shows how much farther the close was from the opening. This means that the prices decreased a lot since the opening and sellers ended up being aggressive. After a decline, a black candlestick shows capitulation or panic.

The Marubozu brothers, White and Black are extremely potent and long candlesticks. Marubozu won't have lower or upper shadows, and you get the lows and highs from the close and open. A White Marubozu is made if the opening is equal to the low, and the closing is equal to the high. This will show the buyers were in control of the action all the way through to the end. Black Marubozu is made if the opening is equal to the high, and the close is equal to the low. This indicates that sellers had control of the action from the beginning trade to the ending trade.

Shadows on candlestick provide significant information for sessions. Uppers are highs and lower and the lows. Candlesticks that have short shadows indicate that most of the actions were close to the opening and closing. Candlesticks with long shadows indicate prices went past the opening and closing.

Candlesticks that have long upper shadows and short lower shadows indicate that buyers had control of the session and bid high. Sellers forced the prices down later from the high, and the close, being weak, made long upper shadows. If a candlestick has short uppers and long lowers, then the sellers were in control of the whole session and ended up making the prices go lower. Buyers came back later to cause the prices to go high near the session's end. Long lower shadows in a strong close.

Spinning tops are when they have a long lower and long upper shadow with a small body. A long shadow indicates a reversal. Indecision is seen in spinning tops. The small body that is either filled or hollow indicates insignificant movement from opening to closing. Bears and bulls were active, which is shown by these shadows. This means the session may have closed or opened with very little change or they could have shifted during the session. If sellers or buyers don't have the upper hand, the result is a standoff. After a long advance, a spinning top indicates weakness with bulls and an interruption of the trend. Once a decline is over, a spinning top shows weakness with bears and an interruption of the trend.

Doji is important candlesticks. They give information by themselves and have components and numbers that create an important pattern. Doji happens if the security opens and closes at the same price. The lower and upper can vary a lot, and this may look like cross or plus sign. By itself, it's mainly neutral. Bias by bulls or bears are based upon previous actions and any confirmation in the future.

Ideally, the opening will be the same as the closing. A doji that has an equal open and close is more robust. You must capture the essence of the candlestick. Doji indicates the indecision between sellers and buyers. Price can move below or above its opening in a session, but they will close at or close to the opening. This will create a standoff. Neither one of the bears or bulls could get control.

Different types of securities may have various criteria for a doji robustness. If a stock is $20, a doji might form with a one-eighth point between opening and closing. A $200 stock might trade for one with a point difference of one and one-fourth point. Figuring out the robustness doji is dependent upon price, excitement, and past candlesticks. In relation to other candlesticks, a doji will be small bodied and a thin line. A doji that formed with other candlesticks that had very little bodies is considered insignificant.

How relevant a doji is will depend on the trends or candlesticks that were before. After an advance, a doji might signal that buying pressure is starting to weaken. After a decline, a doji might signal that any selling pressure is starting to fade. Doji will show that demand and supply are being matched evenly and a trend change may happen. Alone, a doji isn't going to show reversals. Further confirmation will be needed.

After an advance, a doji might signal that pressure is slowing and an uptrend could be ending. Security may decline from not enough buyers. There needs to be pressure for an uptrend. Doji can single and uptrend. After a doji forms, more downside is needed for bearish confirmation. This could be gap at a black candlestick that's long, or a decline under an open of a white candlestick that's long.

After a decline, a doji will show selling pressure is going away, and a downward trend could be near. Even if the bears begin losing control of the decline, more strength will be needed to get a reversal. Confirmation for bullish signals may come from the gap up or advance about the opening. At the end of a doji and long black candlestick traders should look out for a morning doji star.

Long legged doji will have long lower and upper shadows that are equal. These show indecisions with the market. These doji indicates that the price was trade below and above its opening, but closed even to its opening. After much screaming and yelling, the results will show not a whole lot of change from the opening.

Dragon fly doji are made when the close, high, and open are equal, and the low will make long bottom shadows. This candlestick will look like a T. Dragon fly doji show sellers dominated the trading and caused the prices to go lower. At the end of the day, buyers rallied and pushed the price to what it was at opening.

This reversal shows the dragon fly doji depends on future confirmation and previous prices. When the lower shadow is long, it shows buying pressure and the low shows a there were a lot of sellers. After a long downtrend, dragon fly doji indicates a bottom or bullish reversal. When an uptrend ends, the long lower shadow shows a bearish reversal or top. Bullish or bearish, confirmation is still needed for the situation.

Gravestone Doji shows that the opening, low and closing were equal. The high will make a long top shadow. This shows that the T is upside-down with a long top shadow. Gravestone Doji shows that buyers were dominating the trading and drove prices up. By the end, seller rallied and pushed prices down to the opening low.

As with all other candlesticks, what a reversal will do to a gravestone doji depends on what happened in the past. If the upper shadow show that a rally failed, the middle of the day high will show buying pressure. After a long downtrend, the focus turns to show a bullish reversal and buying pressure. When an uptrend ends, the focus will turn at a rally that failed and then bearish reversal. Bullish or bearish, a confirmation will be needed

The candlestick shows the fight between buyers or bulls and sellers or bears over a period of time. Let's use an example of a battle using two different football teams called the Bears and Bulls. The bottom shows a goal for Bears, and tops shows a goal for Bulls. If the end is close to the high, then the Bulls are looking good. If it's closer to the low, then the Bears are looking

Here are six different types of candlesticks:

- Bulls were in control with long white candlesticks.
- Bears were in control with long black candlesticks.
- Prices stayed the same and teams couldn't get control with a candlestick is small.
- Long lower shadows indicate that Bears were winning for some time, but ended up losing control close to the end, and Bulls were able to make a comeback.

- Long upper shadows indicate that Bulls have the first control, but ended up losing it near the end, and Bears were able to make a comeback.

- Long lower and upper shadows indicate that both teams had some good moments during the game, but neither team could get the upper hand on the other and resulted in a standoff.

Candlesticks don't show what happened between the opening and closing just the relationship between the opening and closing. The high and low can't be disputed and obvious, but candlesticks can't indicate which one came first.

With long white candlesticks, everyone thinks that the prices went up during most. This session could have been volatile based on its low and high sequence Candlesticks give important information for the positions of its opening, highs, lows, and closing. This activity makes all candlesticks differ.

CHAPTER 9:

Thing to Know Before You Start

The first thing to consider when getting started in day trading, is which market that you want to use in order to trade. That may sound like an odd question to consider at this point, but depending on how much capital you have, choosing the right market is critical.

The important thing to recognize with day trading is that day traders routinely have strings of losses. And we are not talking about amateurs here, experienced day traders will experience losses on a routine basis.

Of course, you expect that over time you are going to make profits, but just like flipping a penny can result in 5 tails in a row, making many day trades can result in many losses before a big win hit. So, if you're trading a significant amount of your capital, a string of losses could leave you going broke very quickly.

Thousands of dollars can be at stake in an individual trade. For these reasons, there are some rules and recommendations in place to help you avoid getting into super big trouble, but the rules may make day trading seem less appealing especially if you cannot come up with the required capital.

Things to consider before getting started

Day trading isn't a hobby or a game. It's a serious business, and just like any serious business day trading is going to require a serious commitment even before you get started.

- Day trading requires a serious time commitment. You are going to have to study the financial markets, keep up with financial news, and spend time at your computer pouring over financial data. Do you have the time to do all of these things? It's basically a full-time job. You're not going to be a day trader while working your 9-5 and expect to be successful. The day traders who are successful are 100% committed.

- Are you willing to practice before actually beginning day trading? Jumping in and risking tens of thousands of dollars without experience is a bad idea. We have listed links to practice software that lets you simulate stock market trading. Are you willing to spend several months honing your skills using practice methods before actually day trading with real money? You can even open "demo" accounts with many brokers. Consider working on this and practicing now, and then getting into real investing when you've honed your skills.

- Do you have adequate capital to get started? The U.S. government has a $25,000 minimum capital requirement to begin day trading. Do you have the money already? And is this actual money you can lose without getting into serious financial trouble?

Trading on the Stock Market

Of course, you can buy as few or as many shares of stock as you like, but experts advise that you need to have at least $25,000 in the capital that you can risk day trading in order to trade on the stock market. Making four trades in a week will qualify as being a day trader. If you plan to day trade four days per week, it's recommended that you have $30,000, in order to give yourself a bit of a buffer over the minimum. However, this value is quoted on the assumption that you're going to be trading actual shares of stock. It is recommended that your maximum risk on trade be limited to 1% of your total capital.

It's important to know your risk and position risk. Position risk is the number of shares times the risk. If you buy a stock at $20, and the stop-loss is $19, then your risk is $1. If you buy 500 shares, then your position risk is:

500 x ($20-$19) = $500

Stocks with higher volatility will require more risk than stocks with lower volatility. A day trader of stock can access leverage, typically at a rate of 4:1, allowing them to access more shares of stock than they could afford with their own capital.

A good way to get in on day trading on the stock market is --- you guessed it – by trading options. Buying an options contract only requires that you invest in the premium. Trading in options lets you leverage your money.

Futures Markets

You can day trade on futures markets with less capital. This can still let you get involved with stocks, however. For example, you can day trade the S&P 500 on the futures markets with a fraction of the capital required for day trading stocks. You can probably get started on this for between $1,000-$2,500. The daily range of futures can run from 10-40 points depending on volatility.

FOREX Markets

Forex markets are the lowest priced opportunity, with an entry level of capital of about $500. If you are interested in getting into day trading but lack capital, the FOREX markets can be an option to consider in order to get started with day trading. Even though FOREX markets have smaller required minimum accounts, the same rules apply. Traders should not risk more than 1% of their capital on a single trade. If you have a $2,000 account, then the most you'll want to risk on a trade is $20. While FOREX markets might appeal to you because of the smaller minimums, this is an entirely different world, with its own lingo and so forth. That isn't to say that getting some experience in the FOREX markets might be a good idea before risking massive amounts of capital day trading stocks. It very well might be an option to consider in order to use a real testing ground for day trading. FOREX.com, TD Ameritrade, Charles Schwab, and ETrade are recommended brokers for

FOREX. This market will require you to study international trade and to spend time analyzing the global economy, rather than focus on individual companies. It's really a different animal, however, it can be complementary, and many traders do both.

Why Day Trade Options

Day trading stocks have a high barrier for entry because of capital requirements. You may or may not already be in a position to do it, but if you're not trading options provide a low barrier to entry alternative. There are several reasons to trade options rather than stocks. To begin with, trading options don't require hardly any money at all (in comparison) and it will allow you to gain experience looking at many of the same underlying fundamentals that day trading stocks require – since they are ultimately based on the same market.

- Options can be cheap. You can trade options at a much lower premium price as compared to the price required to buy stocks.
- Options offer huge upside potential. The percentage gains in options can be orders of magnitude larger than gains in stocks. So, you can invest a smaller amount of money, and reap larger gains on a percentage basis.
- You don't have to exercise the option to profit from it.
- Volatility makes trading stocks risky; it can make trading options profitable.

- The low price required to invest in options contracts means that you can often put together a diverse portfolio, even when making short term trades.
- It may be harder to get competitive spreads with options while day trading.

There are some downsides to day trading options. One important factor is that when day trading options, time value may limit short term changes in price. Options are also less liquid than the underlying stocks, so that can mean wider bid-ask spreads. Trading options will require you to get the same basic knowledge of day trading that we covered when discussing stocks. Ultimately, the value of the option is determined by the value of the underlying asset – the stock price.

Things to watch day trading options

Let's take a look at some indicators specific to options that you'll want to pay close attention to.

- Put/Call Ratio. If this is high, that means more traders are investing in puts for the underlying asset. In other words, the outlook is bearish because more traders are betting against the underlying or shorting it.
- Money Flow Index. This helps identify overbought and oversold assets. It tells you the flow of money that goes into the underlying asset or out of it over a specified period of time. Money flow takes into account both price and volume.

- Open Interest – this is the total number of outstanding options contracts that have not been settled.
- Relative strength and Bollinger bands Best Tools to Operate Day Trading

Day traders may have special needs to act fast and get information as quickly as possible in ways that normal stock investors don't require. One of the most important things a day trader needs is access to breaking news related to the markets. You're never going to get the kind of detailed and early news that the big players in the institutional investor world will get, but you can still opt for the best options, and that should include Benzinga breaking news.

In addition, some other tools you are going to need:

- Hotkeys, to execute trades quickly.
- Of course, you will need a laptop and a solid internet connection.
- Stock scanning software. Trade ideas are a solid tool:
- eSignal for specialized charting.
- Cable or satellite television, to keep up with ongoing financial news on finance channels like Fox Business and CNBC.
- TAS Market Profile – a software package designed specifically for day traders.

CHAPTER 10:

Factors Influencing day trading

It is not possible to price an option unless an individual understands what constitutes its value. This is because a single option trade can morph into a complex process of adjustments, multiple orders, and several strategies. In the broader sense, options prices are made up of two key components, i.e., time value and intrinsic value.

Time value is any amount that is more than the intrinsic value of the option. The intrinsic value, on the other hand, is the difference between the underlying price of an option and its strike price. Therefore, options that have intrinsic value are those that are in-the-money. This can be summarized as follows:

1. The intrinsic value of a call option = underlying price minus strike price

2. The intrinsic value of a put option = strike price minus the underlying value.

Traders can use options for several different strategies, from high risk to conservative, to achieve objectives that go beyond standard directional strategies. Therefore, it is important to learn and understand the key influencers on options prices in different scenarios. Changes in any or all of these influences will affect the value of an option.

Valuation Models

The valuation model used will affect the price of the options. There is a difference between theories of options pricing and options valuation. For example, the Black-Scholes model and similar pricing models attempt to determine the value of an option in a way that makes it consistent with the price of the underlying security or asset. These theories assume a business environment where a riskless, dynamic arbitrage strategy with the option and stock or asset is possible, thereby determining the option value as an aspect of the arbitrage portfolio.

According to this ideal market environment, if the model value differs from the option's value, the option value can be traded against the number of shares of stock to identify a position that is relatively free of risk. Constant rebalancing will help keep the position free of risk until the expiration date of the option. However, applying these models in real-world trading can prove to be quite challenging, especially if an individual is not adequately experienced in the field of options trading.

In trying to apply any of these theoretical valuation models, a trader will conclude that none of them works as expected. The strategy outlined above, which is supposed to be costless and riskless in theory, is not in practice. This is because positions cannot be continuously balanced when markets are closed. Also, failing to rebalance continuously will lead to transaction costs. These theories also depend on stock volatility, which cannot be predicted exactly.

That said, it is important to understand that these theoretical valuation models offer some valuable assumptions about pricing that are important for options traders to understand; therefore, they should not be taken for granted.

Why Care About How Options Are Priced

In the real world, options prices are determined by supply and demand, like the price of anything else. It is important to understand how options are priced to make smarter and more profitable plays and decisions. To understand how they are priced; options traders need to take note of the following pricing considerations and assumptions based on common valuation theories:

1. The underlying price of an option is normally distributed

2. There are no restrictions to short-selling

3. All securities are desirable and there are no taxes and transaction costs

4. No arbitrage opportunities are risk-free

5. During the life of the derivative asset, there are no dividends

6. For all maturities, the risk-free rate of interest is the same and constant

7. Prices can trade in a continuous manner

Before pilots are allowed to fly, they need to understand what makes an airplane liftoff. In the same way, newcomers into the options trading business need to understand the concepts behind options pricing before investing their hard-earned money into the venture. It can be boring having to learn all the mathematics behind options pricing, but it is worth all the time, effort, and resources spent. Those who neglect to learn how options are priced are likely to fall for shortcuts, which might prove costly in terms of money, time, and effort spent.

It is incredible how some people will take the effort and time to read through the manual of their new Digital TV, but they do not take the time to learn as much as possible about options trading, even with large amounts of money at stake. If options trading were easy, everybody would be doing it. The secret to success is learning how they work and how they are priced. All successful options traders had to learn the math behind options, including pricing methods and key influences on options prices.

Once prospective options traders learn these things, they can better determine whether this field of business is for them. They need to understand volatility backward and forward, up, and down, and understand factors that make or lose money. Essentially, they need to understand the influencers behind every single option price. This is the best bit of advice for novice traders.

Main Influencers on Options Prices

Underlying Asset Price

This is the first influencer on the price of an option. For each underlying asset, there are several options at varying price increments, also referred to as strike price, which is the predetermined price that will apply if the option is exercised. For example, if a trader owns company XYZ stock at $100 per share, he or she could purchase the 100-put since that is where he or she could sell his or her shares in case the company's stock drops in value and he or she decides to exercise the option.

However, an options trader does not have to hold or own shares in a company to trade options; however, the share's strike price will have a significant impact on the option price. For example, for calls, if company XYZ's current stock price is $100 per share, any option that has a strike price higher than $100 is considered to be in-the-money, which is the opposite for put options.

Out-of-the-money options, on the other hand, have no value at expiration. Therefore, if they have no value at the date of expiration, an individual might wonder why it has a value before expiration. It is because the price of stock changes, and there is a good chance that the out-of-the-money options could become in-the-money if there is still some time remaining before expiration.

Volatility

Another factor that goes into options pricing is volatility, which refers to the magnitude of a security's price fluctuations. Extreme volatility leads to extreme price swings and subsequently more risk for stock owners. Different securities have different levels of volatility; however, this fluctuation in price is not constant. This means that a stock that currently has low volatility might become more volatile in the future.

Fortunately, it is much easier to predict volatility than stock price; therefore, options traders need to place themselves on the profitable side of volatility. However, its effect on an option price is one of the most difficult concepts for novice traders to grasp. To determine its effect, a trader needs to look at past stock price movements over a certain period, which is referred to as statistical volatility or historical volatility.

CHAPTER 11:

Choose how to do day trading

Now that the internet and the online trading platforms have made day trading easy for common people, many people think of adopting this as their career choice. There is a misconception among such people that with day trading, they can make easy money. In fact, day trading requires hard work; successful day traders spend hours preparing their trading strategies and doing chart analysis. If you are willing to follow their path, then you too can create a career in day trading.

Your success in this field depends on how you prepare your strategies, and how well you can analyze stock charts. For beginners, it can be challenging initially, but once they get to know the right way of analyzing charts and preparing trading plans, it becomes easy to prepare for day trading.

First comes the technical analysis of stock charts, based on which, trading plans and trading strategies are prepared. Technical analysis is done with the help of many technical indicators. These indicators are used to plot the course of price over various time frames. Based on how the price creates different patterns on technical charts, day traders expect how the price will move in the future. Accordingly, they prepare trade strategies; where they will buy or sell any stock; where they will put a stop loss or book their profits. For day traders, technical analysis is the most important weapon in their arsenal. Since day trading is done within one session of 6 hours, traders must know how the price will move within that short period. If they don't know whether the price will go up or down in the next session, they will cluelessly buy and sell, incurring financial losses and brokerage. Once they have prepared charts; day traders prepare their trading strategies based on the expected price moment. A wide range of strategies is available that can be used for day trading. Traders, who day trade in Options, need specialized trading techniques, which is beyond this book. About Options trading, many books are available online, which day traders can read to learn this specialized skill. The most common strategy for day traders is buying and selling near support and resistance levels. These levels are marked on technical charts and day traders make buying or selling decisions accordingly. Learning technical analysis, creating trading plans and strategies is essential for successful day trading. The internet is full of articles and books about technical analysis and day trading strategies. It is advisable that beginner day traders spend some time learning and getting familiar with these techniques before they trade.

Trading Strategies for Beginners

There are many day trading strategies used by traders. Some of these are conventional, some unconventional; developed by individual day traders. These strategies include different forms of trading and using different technical indicators to find trade entry and exit points.

Scalping is a popular day trading strategy among Forex traders. Here, they trade for a very short time, looking to make small gains but accumulate them through the session.

Some day traders trade by market timings; referring to making use of the opening and closing hours' volatility.

Then there are range traders, who trade when markets are in a sideways trend and move within a definite, horizontal price range. Such traders make use of support and resistance levels to buy at support and sell at resistance (also known as buy low, sell high strategy).

Some traders swear by the importance of news reports, and they trade only on those days when some news report creates a big moment in stock markets.

Nowadays high-frequency trading has become popular where mathematical algorithms used to create trading strategies.

Since there are hundreds and thousands of day traders in stock markets, trading every day, developing one's trading strategy or using the established once becomes essential for success in day trading. With the help of hundreds of technical indicators and various trend theories, individual traders can develop their trading style and strategies. There are different trends in markets and different strategies are used to trade during those times. Based on the trend, these can be directional and non-directional trading strategies.

Directional trading strategies are used when markets are trending in the up or down direction. Trading with the trend line is the simplest directional trading strategy in trending markets. Trending markets can be bullish or bearish. Day traders use different directional strategies for bullish or bearish trends. For example, in a bullish market, day traders try to spot 'higher low' patterns and buy when prices create such a pattern. In a bearish market, day traders locate "lower high" price pattern and sell when such a pattern is formed on technical charts.

Non-directional trading strategies are simple to create because the market creates a series of highs and lows in a sideways trend. Traders draw a horizontal line linking all high points, and one line linking all lows. Then they sell when the price reaches the high-points' line and buy when the price touches the low-points' line.

Markets keep changing trends from time to time. The traders must spot the right trend and use the right strategy for profitable trading. Otherwise, they will only suffer losses. For example, their directional strategy may be correct. However; if they use it in non-directional markets; it will fail and cause them financial loss.

Select and Trade Only a Few Stocks

Your choice of stocks for trading should be aligned with your profit goals in day trading. Different traders have different investment capacities, and based on that, they choose their day trading styles and stocks. Traders who can invest heavy capital, prefer to day trade futures because trading in futures requires a big margin.

Those who are not willing to deposit big money, and, are looking to trade with a small trading capital, opt for intraday trading in options.

There is an in-between category of traders, who buy and sell stocks in cash markets and look to generate profit from the intraday price movement.

Whatever may be your trading style, it is very essential to choose the right stock for trading. Stock exchanges create different categories for stocks of various sectors. So, you will have stocks of all financial companies in one sector and all technology stocks in another. These different sectors also have their separate indexes and have their trading patterns. You will have to do some research about which sectors are moving quickly, then which stocks in that sector have higher liquidity and trading volume. Select just one or two stocks from that sector and focus on them for trading.

Many day traders make the mistake of running after any stock that is making news that day and trade new stocks every day. This is a very fickle trading method and stops them from learning and analyzing the price pattern. This shows a herd mentality; to go where the crowd is going.

Successful day traders carefully choose a few highly liquid stocks, and trade only those stocks, ignoring all others. By doing so, they can fully focus on the analysis of those stocks, which gives them time to become familiar with the trading pattern of a few selected stocks. Stock markets repeat the price patterns at intervals. Therefore, any stock will have its particular support and resistance levels, which it will repeat in its trading pattern. If you follow one stock for many days, weeks or months, become familiar with its trading patterns, it will become easy for you to decide when to buy and sell that stock.

There are thousands of stocks available for trading in stock markets. It is easy to become tempted to buy and sell news-making stocks. But remember, it takes time to know any stock's trading pattern. Unless you are familiar with the price pattern of any stock, you cannot make correct trading decisions about that. Volatility is another criterion for selecting stocks for day trading. Highly volatile stocks are preferred for day trading because the quick fluctuations in its price give day traders a chance to profit from those price movements.

Follow Important Trading Rules

Day trading is not some half hazard activity, but a very systematic and planned method of trading stocks. If you want to become a successful day trader, always remember a few rules and follow them for profitable trading.

The first rule is always to plan your trades. Like cooking a dish. You don't just randomly throw some ingredients together, put them in a cooking pan and create tasty dishes ready to eat. There is always a method and planning involved in cooking. Likewise; all businesses need planning for success, and day trading is no exception.

So, make it a habit of preparing your trading plan the night before. When markets open, you should be ready with a plan of buying, selling, putting a stop-loss, and profit booking levels for that day. The best day trading plan will fail if you don't follow it. Meticulously follow your trading plan, and soon, you will start accumulating profits.

Many day traders who want to leave their 9 to 5 jobs have a misconception about day trading. They assume, this is also a regular hours' job, where they trade for a few hours and earn their salary. If you treat day trading as a job, you will fail. To succeed in day trading, you must treat it as a business. In a job, you do not invest any money. But in business, you invest your own money and try to earn a profit from it. Always remember the rule of treating day trading as a business venture.

When you are investing money in some venture, like in day trading, it becomes your responsibility to protect your money. In day trading also, you must use all rules of money and risk management so that your money is safe. While trading, never leave your positions open without a stop-loss. All professional traders stress this point for a successful day trading. Putting a stop-loss saves your trade from losing money in highly volatile market situations. Another rule of money management is avoiding over-trading.

Always keep count of how many times you have traded in a day because every trade will cost you brokerage.

Another important rule of money management is, investing only the money you can afford to lose. If you have $200 and can afford to lose only $20, then put only that much money in day trading. Never borrow money for trading. Day trading is a business and therefore; here returns are not guaranteed within a fixed period. Never be greedy in intraday trading. Keep small profit targets and exit your trade once you have achieved your targets.

Follow these simple rules for safe and profitable day trading.

Profit-making by Short Selling

When people hear 'day trading', they think of buying stocks; making some profits; and then selling them. But selling first is another method of profitable trading. In trading language, it is called short selling.

Traders indulge in short selling when they have a negative outlook on markets and think the stock prices are going to decline. Short selling is an advanced technique and is not suitable for everyone. Once you have become an experienced day trader; you can start experimenting with short selling in declining markets.

CHAPTER 12:

Develop a Plan

Far too many beginners set themselves up for trouble when they begin trading options by not having a plan. If you want to earn consistent profits when trading options, it is important to have a solid trading plan, and to be disciplined when carrying out your trades. These days, trading options is pretty easy. In some ways, that is a great thing. However, it can also lead people into trouble. If you just trade options on a whim, that can end up leading to quick losses.

Options prices can move fast. A simple moment of thought illustrates what can happen. Since the price of an option could move by $50, $75, or even $90 for a mere $1 rise or decline in the price of a share of stock, it's very easy for options prices to move very quickly. These rapid and dramatic price movements can create a lot of problems for new traders, and if you are only buying and selling individual call and put options, you are going to be very susceptible to these issues. If you were to buy five call options, and the stock price dropped by $1 with a delta of 0.75 over the course of ten minutes, you would lose $375.

And if you get in a situation like that, without a trading plan you won't be sure what to do. Often, stock prices can quickly reverse, and a $1 rise or fall of a stock price isn't all that significant for many of the most popular stocks, that have share prices that range from $100 to $2,000 per share. So, a $1 move in share price is not something necessarily unprecedented.

So, one of the problems with a big drop in price is that panic may ensue, and a novice trader will sell out to cut their losses. This can turn out to be a bad decision in many cases, and so selling options when there is a loss like that is not necessarily something that is the right decision. In this book we will introduce the topic of technical analysis to help you learn ways to determine when to get in and out of trades, but the point here is that you need to have a plan in place rather than trading on emotional impulse.

This can work the other way as well. If the price of a share rises by $1, you could end up with significant gains (for the sake of example and simplicity, we are assuming that you are trading call options). One of the problems that happens with novice traders, is they get overwhelmed with irrational exuberance when share prices are rising. If the share price rises by $1, and you have five call options that rise in value by $345, it's easy to start having visions of making $1,000 in an afternoon. But of course, what often happens is a $1 rise in share price can suddenly turn into a $2 loss, and it can do that in a matter of minutes.

Trading Psychology

To avoid making these kinds of mistakes, it is important to adopt a trading psychology. In short, this means having a strict plan that you follow at all times. In a sense, you need to be detached from your trading on an emotional level, as if you were not the one risking the money. Of course, this is not something that is always easy to do. If you are losing your own hard earned money, it can be difficult to detach yourself emotionally from what's going on.

The way to do this is to setup rules ahead of time and follow them. As a part of your trading psychology, becoming organized and disciplined is going to be something that you need to master. If you are not the kind of person who is organized and prone to detailed planning, then you will need to adjust your approach to things.

An important part of the trading psychology is not giving into emotion. As we mentioned in the introduction, you can fly into a panic when you get large losses, and you can also become excessively elated when you get gains. When you let emotion guide your trading decisions, you are going to find that you make a lot of mistakes. Sometimes, luck will be involved and so traders who are prone to making emotional decisions and not carefully planning out their trades are still going to have some impressive wins. This helps to keep them addicted and bring them back to make many trades, and if they get a big winning trade it will encourage them to keep following the same impulsive process hoping to hit another big win.

The best trading psychology is one that begins with a long-term plan. You should sit down and figure out what your long-term goals are over different time frames. First off, you need to be thinking in terms of reasonable gains. You are not likely to build success by hoping to make a million dollars right away. Instead, think in terms of making $100 a week, or $200 a week. Then map out a strategy that is going to help you actually realize your goals. Then once you have reached the goal, you can set a new goal to increase your income.

Trading options is not something that you can do if you have a "set it and forget it" attitude. As an options trader, although you don't necessarily have to be glued to your computer all day long, you need to be carefully tracking the movements in the share price of any underlying stock for your options. You don't want to impulsively buy an option (or ten options) and then go off and forget about them. You should be checking regularly to see how your options are doing, and possibly using electronic tools to setup alerts and so forth.

Trading Journal

It is my belief that every options trader should keep a written record of their activities in a trading journal. Start the journal by mapping out your goals for the next 3 months. Include the amount of money you want to earn and develop a plan to reach your goal. Then include a record of all your trades in the journal. Include the date you enter the trade, how many options you bought or sold, and the amount of capital involved. Then when you close out your trade update your entries with the final results. It is important to keep a record and be honest with yourself. One of the mistakes that impulsive and emotional traders make is they don't keep a record of their actual trades. That makes it easy to fool yourself into thinking that you are breaking even or even making a profit, when in fact you are losing money.

You should also keep a record of your results, including profits and losses for each trade and any other expenses. This can be kept in written form or by using a spreadsheet. This will help you determine whether or not you have a winning trading program and know your actual net gain or loss. It is important to be realistic about where you are and how well you are doing in reaching your goals, and keeping a detailed record rather than winging it is one way to do that.

If you find that you are constantly having losing trades, then you shouldn't keep doing what you've been doing. Obviously in the beginning you can expect to lose money on several of your first trades possibly, and you might lose money on multiple trades in a row. That is fine in the first few weeks of trading, but if you find after a month you are continually losing money on your trades, you will need to take a step back and do some analysis to find out the reasons why you keep losing on trades. Write down everything about the trade, including how long you stayed in the trade, what made you pick the trade, how much was invested, and so on. Are you holding on too long? Getting out too prematurely? Investing in options right before earnings calls and getting hammered by bad decisions? Getting in on a rising stock price too late, only to find that you mistimed it and the stock price started dropping soon after you entered into your positions?

When you do your analysis and come up with some adjustments to your trading approach, then you can resume trading with an updated training plan. Keep in mind that this is a work in progress, and you don't have to expect success immediately.

Be Realistic: It is not all wins

Many traders think they are not doing well if they don't win on every trade. The reality is that even the best options traders are going to experience losses. The goal is to win more often than you lose so that you have net profits. Over time as you gain experience, you can expect to improve your performance.

Value Education

The fact that you're reading this book is a great sign! Those who are willing to study and learn are definitely going to be more successful than those who simply start trading on impulse. But don't let this book be the end of your education, it should only be the beginning. There are many resources available for those who want to trade options, and you should continually take advantage of them. The more that you can learn about options trading, the more likely it is that you are going to be successful. You should watch as many videos as you can find, learn all the different ways and strategies that can be used when trading options, and read as many books and educational materials as possible.

You should look for official information about options that can help you learn the ropes from experienced traders. Many organizations that are associated with options trading have educational materials available. I also strongly recommend that you follow tasty trade. This is a group associated with the options trading platform Tasty Works, but you don't have to have an account with Tasty Works to use the educational platform. They have a large number of educational videos which are free to view on their website and on YouTube. They also have talk shows where they discuss different trading results, approaches to trading, and interviews with people who became successful options traders. Since it's free and put together by people who have been professional options traders for many decades in some cases, this is one of the best resources that you can use to educate yourself about trading options.

Use Buying and Selling Calls as a Learning Opportunity

Many novice traders have visions of making millions of dollars buying and selling individual call options. It is possible to make money trading individual call and put options, however very few professional traders make a career doing so. The fact is that straight trading of individual options is not likely to bring consistent and long-term success. It is just too difficult to consistently predict which way a stock price is going to move over short time periods.

CHAPTER 13:

Learn to Manage Risks of Day Trading

If you want to be successful at day trading, there are three things that you need to have. You need to have a sound psychology that can handle the stress of this trading style, a set of trading strategies that will help you make good decisions, and a good plan to help you manage your risk. If you are missing out on one of these parts, your whole program will fail, and you will not make money with day trading.

As a beginner, it is easy to focus only on the trading strategy that you are using. While the trading strategy is pretty important, it leaves you without the other three components that are just as important. Just because you have picked out a good strategy to work with does not mean you have the right self-discipline to stick with that strategy or to wait the market out long enough, and this could be the reason that you are failing, regardless of the strategy that you pick.

There will be plenty of time for the strategies that you can use later, but for now, we need to learn some of the rules that you must follow to manage your risk. Of course, any strategy that you pick will have times when they will lead to a bad trade. The market does not always behave the way that it should or that we expect. But when you learn to manage your risk, you will not lose out as much money as you would just jumping into the market.

The first thing that you should do to manage your risks is to draw a line in the sand or have an exit point when you will decide it is time to get out of the trade. Pride can be hard to swallow for a lot of people, and they may find that it is hard to admit defeat or that they were wrong about a trade. But holding onto that trade will simply lead you to losing more money and will make the mistake bigger than before. You need to learn when to cut your losses and then walk away.

There will be times when the trade goes against you. This happens to beginners as well as to those who have been in the market for a long time. When the trade starts to go against you, it is time to exit. It is common in day trading for the unexpected to happen all of the time because there are such big fluctuations in the market from one moment to another. It may be hard to admit the defeat, but remember that there are always other trades that you can do on other days.

Your main job in day trading is to make money. If you are holding onto a position that is going against you just because you want to be able to prove that a prediction you made was right, then you are a bad trader. Your job here is not to always be right; it is to make money.

Another thing that you should do to minimize your risks is always to follow the plans and rules of your chosen strategy. This will be really easy when the trade is going well, and you are making money. But when you are in the middle of a bad trade, you may be tempted to go against those rules. This may seem like a good idea at the time, but it can end up costing you a lot of money. Following the rules of your strategy may make you lose a bit of money, but it is much easier to lose a little and get back into the game later than to end up with a big loss. It is better to take some of those quick losses, get out of the trade, and then come back to it all later on.

Next, you need to make sure that you are finding low-risk entries that can provide you with a high potential reward. These can be risky still, but they pose a lot less risk than you will find with other stocks that you choose. The best setup is when you find an opportunity that will provide you with a trade that has a very little risk. For example, risking $100 to make $300 is a good setup, but if you are risking $100 to make $10, you are in the wrong trade. Most expert traders are not going to work on trades that have a ratio of less than 2 to 1 for profit-to-loss.

What this means is that if you purchase $1000 of stock and you are risking $100 on that stock, it is important that you sell that stock for a minimum of $1200 to make it worth your time and to decrease the risk. Of course, it may not always work out that way, and you may need to accept a loss, such as when the stock goes down to $900, but there should at least be the potential to make $1200. If the potential is only to make $1100 on the stocks, the profit-to-loss ratio is too low, and you should not risk it.

On some days, you are not going to be able to find a stock that has the right profit-to-loss ratio. That is fine. It is much better to stay out of the market for a day than to trade on a stock that does not provide the requirements that you need. You can enter the market later on, on another day or two down the line, knowing that you did not risk your money in the process. With the 2 to 1 ratio, you will be in a good position. Remember that there are still going to be times when you are wrong, or the market goes the opposite way than it should. If you stick with this ratio or better, you can still be wrong 40 percent of the time and make money from day trading.

The three questions to ask

Whenever you decide to purchase a stock on a trading platform, you are risking some of your money. Even stocks that fit into the ratio that we talked about before can run into some issues, and you have to realize that you are risking your money each time that you do this. However, there are some steps that you can take to manage this risk. The questions that you should ask yourself before any of your chosen trades include:

• Am I trading with the right stock: the first step of risk management is to work with the right stock? If you pick out the wrong stock, it does not matter what tools or platform you are using, you will end up losing. You need to make sure that you are avoiding stocks that do not have any movement, penny stocks that can be highly manipulated, ones that have a small trading volume, and those that are already being traded heavily by institutional traders and computers.

• What share size should I work with: the next question is to decide how many shares you should purchase. This will depend on how much money you have available and your daily goals. If you only want to hit a target of $1000 each day, then you will need to purchase more than 20 shares in most cases. If you do not have enough money in your account for this kind of target, then it is time to lower the daily goal.

• What is my stop loss: this is basically the amount that you are comfortable with losing if the market goes south. The most that you should never risk more than two percent of the equity in your account. This means if you have an account that holds $10,000, you should not risk over $200. This means that you may not make as much of a return on investment on your trades, but also helps you to keep most of your money in your account.

The three-step risk management plan

Step 1: the first step that you should take is to determine the absolute maximum dollar risk that you will take for the trade you are planning. It is recommended that as a beginner, you should never risk more than 2 percent of the equity in your account, but you can choose to go up and down from this number based on how much money you have and how much you are willing to risk. You need to have this amount calculated before you even start trading for the day.

Step 2: the second step is to estimate the maximum risk per share that you will take, the strategy stop loss, from your entry. We will learn more how to do this later because you will have a different stop loss based on the strategy that you choose.

Step 3: take the number from step 1 and divide it by the number you got from step two. This will give you the maximum number of shares that you can trade each time. Do not go about this level, or you are increasing your risk too much.

Let's take a look at how this would work. Let's say that you will get some stocks and you have $40,000 in your account. If you stick with the rule of only using 2 percent, then you would limit your risk to $800. We will be conservative for this trade as beginners and only risk 1 percent of the account, or $400. Now we have finished step one.

As you are monitoring the stock, you see that a situation is developing where you would use the VWAP Strategy to get the best results. So you decide to sell the short stock when it reaches $50, and you want to cover them at $48.80, with a stop loss at $50.40. This means that you will be risking about $0.40 per share. This will be step 2.

Now we are moving on to step three. We will calculate our share size by dividing the numbers in step 1 and step 2, so we can find the maximum size that we can trade. For this example, we would be able to purchase a maximum of 1000 shares.

Now, with the money that you have in your account, you may not have the right buying power to get the shares at $50. So, you would choose to purchase fewer shares, such as 500 shares to get started with. With the strategies that we have talked about, you are never allowed to risk over 2 percent, but you can always be conservative and riskless.

CHAPTER 14:

Skills You Must Have

When it comes to trading anything, there are several skills that you must have in order to help you complete your trades, or complete your trades better. In any case, you should always be looking into opportunities for you to learn how to become a better trader so that you can increase your profits and minimize your risks. The more educated you are, the more aware you can be of how certain things may influence your trades, and therefore the better your trading can become.

Some of what you are going to learn when you begin trading will come through hands-on experience and truly cannot be taught to you by another individual. You will find that your own instincts around whether or not a trade is going to be a good deal will refine and improve as you go, making it easier for you to find the best trade deals for you to engage in.

With that being said, others can certainly be taught to you so that you know what to look out for or how to complete certain parts of your trade deals with greater confidence and success. To help you get started, we are going to look into the skills that you need to have in order to become a better trader, and how you can employ these skills in your own trades.

How to Place an Order

Placing an option order may seem intimidating at first, especially if you are not used to the platform that you are trading on. If you have never traded anything in the past, the brokerage platform you use, regardless of which one, can seem pretty foreign. Rest assured, getting started with placing orders is not as hard as it may seem and your brokerage platform will start to make a lot more sense to you after you have placed your order. The only way you can really begin to navigate and learn about your platform is to begin using it, so you will need to make these first steps in order to really get the hang of things. With that being said, you can (and should) always start with more conservative trades in the beginning so that you can give yourself some time to understand the platform that you are using and make your trades accordingly.

The first thing you need to do is log into your brokerage account, as this is where you are going to see the opportunity to make your purchases. Depending on how your brokerage works, you may need to log into a certain website or download an application and log in there to get started. In either scenario, make sure that you are following the right steps for your platform so that you can get into your account.

Once you are logged into your account, you are going to see either a page or a tab, depending on what brokerage you are using, that says "trade" or "order." This page or tab should be clearly labeled since this is the entire purpose of the platform, so it should not be too challenging for you to miss. Go to that page.

Now, you want to pull up a quote for the stock or ETF that you are going to be trading.

Side Note: ETFs, or exchange-traded funds, are just another form of financial instrument that can be traded. ETFs are a type of financial instrument that essentially groups together various stocks into a "basket" type of fund, allowing you to invest in that single fund rather than investing in each individual stock being represented by the fund. Every ETF is already created with pre-determined stocks, so you will not be choosing the stocks in the ETF, just the ETF that is filled with the types of stocks you want to be trading in. In many cases, ETFs can be less risky to trade than open stocks, so they tend to be more ideal for beginners or those looking for a more conservative trading opportunity.

After you have located the quote for the stock or the ETF, you will see what the stock is currently trading at and how it has changed in the recent past. You will also see how much people are generally paying for the options relating to this stock, and how much people are generally asking for. These numbers fluctuate constantly as the market prices change, so you will need to get a new quote every single time you want to trade, even if you are trading the same stock.

Under the quote, you have identified, or somewhere on the quote screen, you should see what is known as an "options quote table." It may simply say "options" which will lead you to the same table. On that table, you will see what options are currently available for sale around this particular stock, as well as what parameters each option is created with.

When you open the table, the first thing you want to do is select your expiration month so that you are only viewing options that are going to continue to exist for as long as you need them to.

Then, you want to select your strike price from the options that are available with your chosen expiry date. Make sure that you are looking at options that are reflective of the type of option that you want to buy, meaning that if you want to purchase a put option you are looking at put options, and if you want to purchase a call option you are looking at call options.

You do not want to accidentally purchase the wrong type of option for the strategy you are looking at trading with. Typically, call options are on the left side of the table and put options are on the right side of the table.

Once you have located the option you want to purchase and verified that it is the right type, has the right expiry date, and features the right strike price, you can go ahead and enter the quantity for how many options you want to buy. Then, you need to set the price for how much you want to pay for the options that you are purchasing.

Next, you will choose what type of order you want to purchase. As a general rule of thumb, you should only order "limits" when you are trading options. The additional seven styles are more advanced and can be learned about later, once you have mastered the basics of options trading. For now, let's keep it simple.

The last thing you are going to need to do before you confirm and send the order is choose whether you want to purchase a day order or a GTC order, or a "Good 'Til Cancer" order. You will want to pick day orders, as these are the orders that will be relevant for your day trading style. For day orders, they will cancel automatically when the market closes, whether or not you have exercised the order. If the order cancels, this means it closes and you no longer have the option to purchase the stocks represented by the order itself.

After you have set all of these parameters in place, you can confirm your order and send it. You should always double-check everything to ensure that you have filled out your order properly, to avoid having any accidental mistakes that may cost you later on.

At this point, the funds required to purchase the order will be removed from your brokerage account and invested into the option.

How to Close an Open Order (Before the Expiration Date)

As a day trader, the options that you open are going to cancel by the end of the day, which means that you need to be paying attention to them and trading on them before the day ends. You do not want your options to cancel before you have exercised them unless you are intentionally letting them expire worthless, as this may result in you missing out on opportunities to earn profits. For this reason, you are going to need to check-in and conduct your trades throughout the day to prevent your losses.

There are two ways that you can close an option order: buy to close, or sell to close. Both of these strategies are going to afford you the opportunity to close your option position, hopefully with profits from it, and end the day in the money.

It is important that you know how to use both of these strategies as each one will help you increase your profitability from the position you are leveraging. With that being said, you should always have a general idea of how you are going to close your option before you go into your trade to avoid being caught in a trade with no clear idea as to how you are going to profit from it. In other words, never trade without a clear action plan for how you are going to open, manage, and close your trade.

Buy to Close Your Option Trade

Buying to close means that you are exiting your short position by buying the asset that is being represented by your option. In this position, your profits are going to be gained if you purchase the asset itself, meaning that you want to exercise the option and take ownership over those stocks.

This means that when the market closes you will now have possession over the stocks that you were trading.

Buying to close your option trade is simple, you will open your brokerage platform and log in and then locate the open orders that you are currently holding. You will then locate the open order you want to act on, enabling you to see how that order is performing and any information relating to that particular contract. You will also see the option to "exercise" the option or "buy" the stocks that the option represents. Select this and your trading platform will provide you with the step-by-step guidance on how to purchase these stocks from your contract, based on how your unique platform works.

Sell to Close Your Option Trade

Sell to close options is a strategy where you do not want to buy the underlying asset but you do want to close your position. In this case, you will sell the option contract you are currently holding to someone else so that they can hold the contracts instead, and you are no longer in the position of possessing them. In this situation, no stocks are traded and you will not receive any shares in the underlying asset because you are selling the contract, or the option, to buy them.

You forfeit the right to exercise your contract in this scenario, meaning that you will only recover or profit from the premium paid to you by another investor when they buy your contracts.

Sell to close can be exercised whether you are in a short or long position. Generally, your goal here is to either profit from the price of the premium or recover the price you paid on your premium. You may or may not end up with a small gain from this trade when you are done.

CHAPTER 15:

How to open a brokerage account?

To execute the trades that you want, you will need to open up a brokerage account. There are varieties of factors that are going to come into play when you pick out a brokerage account including the margin rates, the commissions you will pay, and any other applicable fees. If you pick a terrible broker or one who takes too many fees from you, it doesn't matter how successful you are with your trades; they will end up taking most, if not all, of the profits that you make.

If you plan to be a high-volume trader, you could end up paying a ton of commission fees each day to the broker. For those who plan to trade in high volume which is more common with day trading compared to other forms of trading, you will need to contact your broker to gather information about the brokerage rates. Make sure to ask about all their fees, any incentive plans or offers so as to save yourself from flight of hard-earned profits.

After you have a good idea about the costs and fees you will have with a broker, you will need to take a look at the platforms they have to offer. These platforms are significant because they could affect things like price quotes and execution speed for your trades. As a day trader, even a few seconds of delay in the processing can cost you a lot of money. Many brokers will have executions that happen in real time but there are times when slippage can happen. You should test out the brokerage's platform to see if it is comfortable and if you like the way it works.

Take some time to look at the financial stability and customer service of the brokers you are considering. You want to pick out a brokerage firm that has great customer service because if a crisis happens, you would need to exit quickly from the market. Financial strength can be important because there are brokers who have gone out of business, and if yours does, it may cost you the entire amount that is in your account.

There are many different brokers you can consider using for your trading needs. Some of the best ones that you may want to work with include:

- MB Trading
- Speed Trader
- Generic Trade
- Options press
- E-Trade
- Fidelity
- TD Ameritrade
- Lightspeed

- Trade Station
- Interactive Brokers

After you have selected the broker you want to work with, you can set up your account, and add money. Most brokerage firms will require you to have money in your account before you even start with any trades. Take some time here to explore all the features that come with your new trading account, checking out the different graphs, the interactive tools, etc. Then, when you are ready, you can start using your strategy to make money with day trading.

When you are setting up your brokerage account, you need to make sure that you watch out for some of the fees that you incur. Each brokerage account, even if you do most of the work by yourself, is going to charge some fees for doing the trades. You need to know what all of these are before you even think about trading, or you could lose all your profits in the form of payment for brokerage charges.

Some brokerage accounts will charge a base fee for each trade that you do. This can often get expensive especially since day trading relies on you being able to do a ton of little trades throughout the day. This is often not the best option in fees to go with unless you are a long-term trader who doesn't plan to get out of the market for a long period. Most day traders will go on a commission basis, so they only have to pay when they make a profit. When working out your strategies, make sure to factor in the fees or the commissions that you have to pay, and take those out of your profits when determining how profitable a trade is.

The Importance of the Right Time and Timing

Understanding the right time to trade is very important. Investing money at the right time is one of the most determining factors for the success of your investment. The fundamental concept remains the same: how and when to place a trade for making profit in the stock market.

To make sure that you know, in advance, how much you can earn and how to make money for us, you cannot rely on chance. Above all, we cannot expect to waste time and thus the money by making unnecessary mistakes in the market.

Everything has its time; also, in investment, they have their right times and their importance. As you can see, even the right timing serves to give way to the investment, to make your cycle, and to express that reasonable expectation. The right setup also serves your capital to survive in any situation, resist negative moments, and always have the strength to start again.

Avoiding Risks

To better understand the risks involved in trading in risky stocks, it seems right to remember the right principles. Suppose you can trade $10,000 in a strategy that has 50% risk. This strategy was put in place to increase the capital by a multiple of three through trading profit. It is a highly risky strategy from our point of view as it could result in the total loss of the entire capital. This operation is recommended only to experienced traders.

With this example, we have made you understand how these operations allow you to double or triple the capital within a few months but also how you can lose all your capital in a matter of months. In fact, by implementing these dangerous strategies, you will also see the account being halved, or entirely burned, within a few weeks.

To understand everything more effectively, let's take another example. According to your trading strategies, you have traded on a particular asset with a strategy and think that this can give you a return of 50% within a month.

To not fall into error, we advise you to set the opposite goal or try to ask the question: how would it be if in half a month you lost half of the amount? We believe that you must have understood in a simple and fast way as to what is the significance of the right time for trading. This way you can also learn to avoid wrong trading strategies.

Limiting Damages of Social Trading

Many wonder if social trading is the right strategy to avoid wasting time and earning. Before proceeding, we remind you that social trading is not a risk-free form of trading, even if the risk, in this case, is reduced. To trade in social trading, we believe it is essential to operate for some time between 9 and 12 months minimum. This is for one simple reason. Before choosing an investment system, you must see the performance for at least a year. In this sense, there is no need to follow a trader, 24 hours a day, 365 days a year. You only have to examine all the data of all the operations performed during the year, perhaps with the help of special tools that simplify reading.

Once you have understood how to trade, how much trading exposure can you take and what stock you want to trade in, you have to consider the risk that you are willing to take. Beyond this limit, it is advisable to leave it alone.

In most cases, the conditions that have led you to make a certain investment choice must have solid foundations so that the investment can yield good profits. A trading experience of almost one year will be good enough to make you understand if your investment decisions are right or wrong.

CHAPTER 16:

Options Strategies for Unchanging Prices: The Iron Condor and Iron Butterfly

A lot of the focus in introductory treatments of options is on buying calls or puts to take advantage of rising or falling stock prices. However, these kinds of options trades suffer from one major weakness – having to predict the direction of a price move.

Of course sometimes this is possible within reasonable bounds. You can learn subjects like technical analysis, chart signals, trending, and candlestick charts to make fairly reasonable estimates of price-movements of stock. However this is still fairly risky activity, in the sense that you are just as likely to be wrong as you are to be right in many cases. There are some options traders that do trade straight call options, but most professional options traders do not approach the markets in this way.

That is because while you can strike gold sometimes, it's hard to do it day in and day out. The main weakness in the equation is predicting the direction of a stock price move. But what if we approach options trading in a new and different way, and instead of doing that, remove the directional movements entirely? There are a few different strategies that can be used to do this.

There are also many different situations that occur in the stock market. After an earnings call, the stock can move high or low by large amounts in one direction. As you may know, this usually depends on whether or not earnings "beat" or fail to beat expectations. To be completely honest, this is a bit absurd. If the analysis believe a certain amount of profit is going to be made in a given quarter, but the company makes profit but it's less profit than was projected, this is considered a major "disappointment" and it can cause stock prices to drop by a large amount. If the company happens to beat these imaginary expectations, then stock prices can be sent soaring.

But at other times, the stock is going to be trapped within a range of prices. This can happen for long time periods. The range might be quite constrained, and so it can be hard to make profits by trading calls and puts when the stock is in this pattern. But it turns out that the ability to have calls and puts together enables us to come up with schemes that can earn profits in unexpected ways.

The Iron Condor

The first type of trade that we are going to look at is called an iron condor. This is something you want to apply when the highs and lows of stock prices seem to be bounded. It is as if the stock price is trapped. It never breaks above a certain pricing level, called resistance. But it never drops below a given price level, which is called the support.

Sometimes stock can be trapped in this pattern for a long time period. It will look something like this:

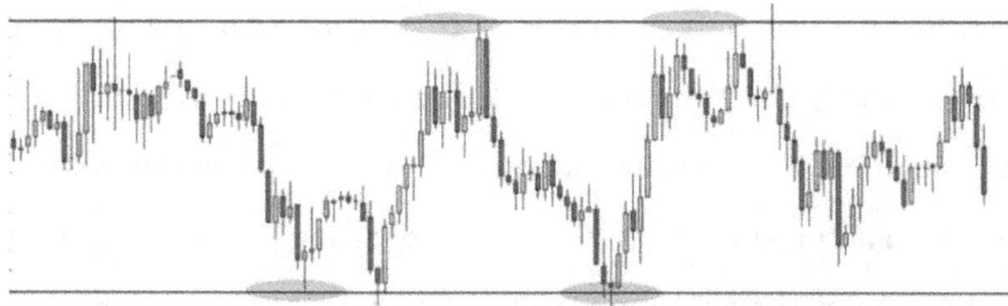

In order to have support and resistance, you want to see the price touch the line of support at least two times, and the line of resistance at least two times. The difference in prices might be relatively small. Of course, there are some possibilities for trading calls and puts, when the price drops down to the support level, you can buy call options and take profit as the price goes back up toward the resistance price level. Then you can buy put options and sell them when the price drops back down to support.

But there is another way to profit from this kind of price trap, as I like to call it. This type of trade is called an iron condor. Among options traders looking to earn an income, the iron condor is one of the most popular ways to trade. If you set it up correctly, it's possible to earn repeated income.

Let's take a minute for an important aside before we show you how to setup the trade. There are two kinds of options traders. One type of options traders is a profit seeking trader. Of course all traders hope to make profits, but a profit seeking trader is one who makes bets on what the stock is going to do, and they roll the dice and gamble hoping to make profits.

The other type of options trader is an income trader. This type of options trader seeks to minimize risk and setup trades so that they can earn regular income from the markets. There are many different ways to do this, and most of them involve selling rather than buying options. When you are a regular options trader, you buy to open your positions. So you are going to be running your business buying low, and selling high in order to make profits.

An income trader sells to open their positions. They seek to make money selling options and while you have been concerned about things like theta and time decay so far, as an income trader you actually value time decay and can't wait for options to expire.

An iron condor is the first type of strategy that we are going to consider that works in this fashion. When you trade an iron condor, you are going to sell it to open your position. Then you are going to make money from the time decay. As long as the stock stays within the range that you use to define the iron condor, you will earn a profit. If it moves outside the range of the iron condor, then you are going to lose money.

So let's see how its setup. The idea of an iron condor is to set boundaries on the stock price, so we are going to be looking for a ranging stock price as shown in the graph above. To set upper bounds, we are going to use call options. The lower bounds of the range are going to be set by using put options.

A single iron condor isn't going to make you a huge amount of money. The basic philosophy behind it is that this is a limited risk – limited profit type of trade. It eliminates having to guess which direction the stock is going to move, and instead we are only going to estimate the bounds of stock price movement over the lifetime of the option. Under normal conditions this type of bet is going to work in most cases. Of course, if there is unexpected news, such as bad news coming out about the company, that can cause prices to move outside the bounds of the iron condor and turn the trade into a loser. Unexpectedly bad news about the economy or political situation can have the same effect.

When volatility is high that means stock prices are swinging between high highs and low lows. Since we are looking for a situation where stock prices are basically bounded in a narrow range of prices, that means that an iron condor is a type of trade you want to use when volatility is relatively low.

To create an iron condor, we are going to trade 4 options at once. We are going to sell two options and buy two options. First let's look at the high price range for the trade. First, we want to sell a call option with a lower strike price. The strike price used for the call option sets the upper boundary of the iron condor. So you are setting this up with the belief that the stock price is not going to exceed the strike price of the call option that you select.

Second, we are going to buy a call option that has a higher strike price than the first call option. This is done because we are going to use it to hedge our risks a little bit. Let's see how that would work. For our example, we will assume that the stock price is $200.

We could sell a call option with a strike price of $205. This means we are setting up our iron condor with the belief that from now until the expiration date of the option, the price of the stock is not going to rise above $205. If there are 30 days to expiration, and volatility is a relatively low 15%, the price of a call option with a $205 strike price is going to be $1.55.

The breakeven price is found by adding the cost of the call option to the strike price, which would give $206.55. As long as the share price stays at $206.55 or below, it's not worth it for the option to be exercised. However, if the share price goes above that value, the option can be exercised. In the case of a call option, as the options seller, this means that you have to sell 100 shares of stock at the strike price of $205 a share.

So how would that work in practice? The way it actually works is your broker buys the shares at the market price, sells the shares to the counterparty to the option contract to close the transaction at the lower strike price, and then they stick you with the losses. So if the share price were $208, you would have a $3 loss per share, or a total loss of $300 for each contract that would cover 100 shares of stock.

Of course stock prices can rise to any value, at least in theory. So you could be getting into real trouble if the stock price rose much higher.

The iron condor caps maximum losses by including a second call option, with a higher strike price. You buy this call option, which means you cap possible profits because you have this added expense. But besides limiting possible profits, it will also cap possible losses.

Since you are buying a call option, you can exercise your rights on that option and buy shares of stock at that strike price that you can sell at the higher market price to make up for some of the loss.

Using our price setup, we could choose $210 as the second strike price. Suppose that the stock price rises to $212. In this situation, the first option with the $205 strike price is going to be exercised. So we have to buy shares at $212 and then sell them to the counterparty of the $205 option at $205 a share, giving us a net loss of $7 a share.

But now we can exercise the second call option that we have purchased. In this case, we buy shares of stock at $210, but then we sell them on the market for $212, giving us a net $2 a share. This helps mitigate the total losses, reducing the total loss to $5 a share, or a total loss of $500. The loss is capped. It's going to be the difference between the two strike prices chosen for our options.

CHAPTER 17:

The Long Straddle/Strangle Strategy

Another strategy that you can work with is the long straddle and strangles strategy. This strategy is nice because it has the potential to make the trader unlimited amounts of profit but there is a limited amount of risk. You have to make sure that you are picking the right kind of stock to make this strategy work. For example, this is a good strategy to work with if you feel your chosen stock is going to deal with a lot of volatility in the near future.

Compared to the other strategies that we have talked about so far in this guidebook, the long straddle is considered one of the riskiest strategies and you will only want to work with it if you feel the movement in your stock or your index is going to be pretty big over the near future.

However, even though there is some risk that comes with this strategy, it does have the potential to help you earn the maximum amount of profits compared to some of the other strategies as well. This is because there isn't an upper limit on the amount of profit that you are able to make when you are working with the long straddle while the other strategies will have a limit on the profit.

There is also the long strangle. This one is similar to the long straddle but there are some modifications that make it slightly different.

So, to execute the long straddle is going to be a bit different than what you were able to do with some of the other strategies that we have talked about. First, pick out the stock that you would like to do. To see success, you need to pick out a stock that is going to show a lot of volatility along the way in the near future, or you are not going to get good results.

After you have chosen the stock that you want to work with, you need to purchase an ATM call option of this stock. Then you need to purchase an ATM put option that has the same stock and the same expiry date as the call option that you purchased in the previous step.

When you complete the purchases, you will want to watch your trade pretty closely. When you see the large price movement that you were watching out for, it is time to close the legs at the same time. This is another strategy that is going to have to fight against the time decay issue and this time decay is going to impact both options, so it is best to not hold onto this kind of strategy for over a few days.

One thing to note is that the strike prices of both your put and your call options need to be the same when doing the straddle trade. This can be difficult to do when entering into a trade though and you may not be able to purchase the options when the market price of the stock isn't matching up to your chosen strike price. When doing this trade, you may find that the market price of your chosen stock might end up being slightly above or below the chosen strike price of your option. This implies that you have a likelihood of ending up with one option that is slightly OTM and the other one ends up being slightly ITM when you initiate this kind of trade. This is fine as long as you keep them as close to ATM as possible.

The long straddle and strangle is a strategy that you are only supposed to use on rare occasions and only when you think that there is going to be a sudden and big rise or fall in the stock you want to choose, usually following some external factor. Even in this kind of trade, when you enter into the long straddle position, you want to make sure that the volatile still isn't too high. Most traders are going to stick with a stock or an index that is less than 60%of historical volatility. The reason that you want to be careful with this is because if there is a big drop in the volatility of the stock, even after the price movement goes the way that you want, this drop-in volatility is going to end up harming how much profit you can make.

Ideally, the long straddle can be traded when there is a big decision making or policy change in the company, especially one that will have a big impact on the stock for that company and that could cause it to fall or rise really quickly over a few days. Some of the situations that may result in conditions being right for the long straddle include:

- The quarterly or annual results from a company will come out in the next few days and people have some big expectations from these.

- A big decision regarding the company that owns the stocks is going to come out soon. This could include a decision for the company to change their management or to do a merger with another company.

- A big announcement that will talk about a large dividend or a bonus issue is going to come out soon.

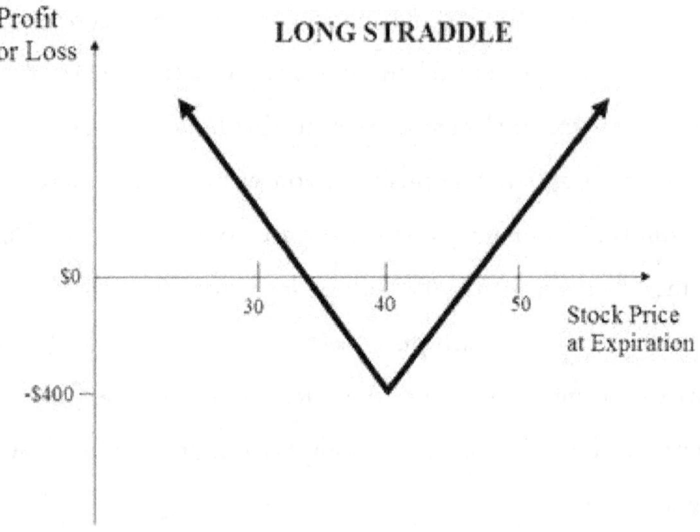

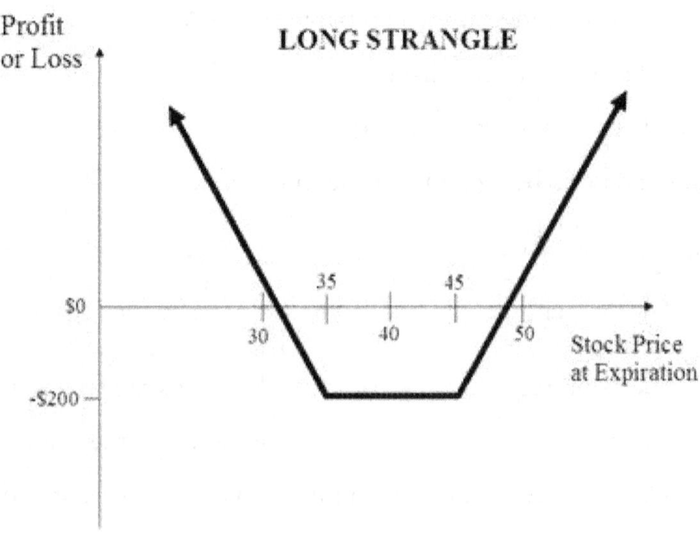

If you are working with a benchmark index, there are many situations that could make it rise or fall. Some of these would include the announcements of the annual budget for the company, when the company is going to make some new monetary policy decisions when there are some major elections in the management of the company, and even some major socio-economic decisions. If you see that any of these are going to happen with the underlying stock, it may be time to work with this position.

On the other hand, if you see that your chosen stock is trading on a pretty narrow range, or if you feel that the outlook on that stock is pretty neutral (without much movement even if it is negative or positive) over the short-term, then the long straddle strategy is not the right one for you. It should also be a strategy that you avoid if the volatility is high, even if there is some potential for movement.

When you get into the long straddle position, it is a good idea to exit this position once you see that there is a big rise or fall in your position and you are gaining profit. It is common for many people to stay in the market too long with this strategy and if you hold onto that position too long, you could end up losing any profits that you earn, thanks to the potential of a drop in volatility or because of the time decay issue.

The primary advantage that you are going to see when working with the long straddle is that you do have the potential to earn unlimited profits as soon as the trade crosses pass the break-even point, no matter what direction it goes in. the straddle is often used to earn profits even when a stock is volatile in the market without having to worry about predicting which direction that the stock will move in and for how long. Volatile stocks often go up and down pretty quickly and it is hard to figure out which way you should go. With this strategy, you will have the opportunity to profit from a rise and a fall of your stock based on the points that you pick.

Another benefit that you can find with the straddle position is that it will limit how much risk you are exposed to. The amount of risk that you will face is the total amount of premium that you paid when you decided to enter into the trade with this stock.

The biggest disadvantage that comes with using the long straddle is that you will have to deal with the time decay issue. In fact, the time decay issue could affect both sides of your straddle trade, the call, and the put, so this issue is compounded and can cause you more issues than you would have with other strategies.

Another disadvantage of using this kind of position to earn a profit is that it can be a bit difficult. In order to earn a profit, you need to properly predict that your chosen stock is going to have a very sharp movement, either up or down, in a pretty short amount of time.

The long strangle

Before we take a look at how to make this strategy work, we also need to take a look at what the long strangle is all about. This strategy is very similar to the long straddle but instead of purchasing an ATM call and put with the same strike price, the trader will choose to purchase a slightly OTM put and call for the same stock and the same expiration date.

The advantage of going with this long strangle rather than the long straddle is that the amount of premium that you will have to pay for your premiums will be less than what you have to pay with the long straddle. However, for the long strangle to work, you are going to need the move in the market to be much bigger in order to recover your costs.

Traders are going to profit using the long strangle any time that they see a sharp move in their stock, similar to using the long straddle position, and you still have the potential to make unlimited profits. However, with this strategy, the maximum loss is going to happen if the price of the stock settles between the strike price for the call and the put when you reach the time of expiry. The maximum loss though, in both the straddle and the strangle, will be the premiums that you paid for the put and the call options.

CHAPTER 18:

Selling Naked Options

Earlier, we have seen two straightforward ways to sell options. You can sell covered call options or sell put options but deposit enough capital into your account in order to cover the cost of buying the shares at the strike price in the event that this becomes necessary.

The second method that we looked at was selling a credit spread, either the put or call types of spread. Although this may be a great income strategy, you are going to reduce the potential profits made by having to purchase out of the money options to mitigate the risk.

Selling Naked Requires Level 4 Status

In order to sell naked options, you must have level 4 trading status. That means that you are going to be required to have a margin account. As we stated earlier, you must deposit $2,000 in order to open a margin account. But for now, the two things to note are that you need to have level 4 trading status and a margin account. You will have to open a margin account before you request level 4 trading status from your broker. They may also require that you have some more substantial trading experience with options, having spent some time as a level 2 and a level 3 trader.

The Put Option Strategy

The goal of selling naked options is to earn regular income. So, you are going to be earning options premium and hoping that the options expire without worth. The method is a little bit simpler than trading put credit spreads because you are not going to have to think about a second option. There is only one option that is involved in this trade.

The trick is to pick an option with a strike price that is out of the money, and out of the money by a large enough margin to more or less guarantee that you are going to end up profiting on the trade. Traders tend to look at one standard deviation below the current share price to find a strike price that is suitable to guarantee profits. Of course, you can never guarantee profits. A sudden news item or another event can send stock prices dropping. But under most circumstances, if you go one standard deviation below the current share price, you can set up a situation where it is likely you can profit from the trade.

As we mentioned earlier, brokers will be providing the chance or probability of earning profits from selling any given option. You can choose a value of 70% or higher for this purpose. If you go further out of the money, the chance for profit increases, but you are going to be earning smaller amounts per trade. Depending on how much profit you are hoping to make, you are going to have to enter into more trades.

Looking at Facebook, an option with 70% of profit has a strike price of $185 and sells for $453. The share price is about $190. If we go to 75%, then we are looking at a strike price of $180 and a sale price of $293.

Either way, you can see that you can build up a significant income by selling put options. Of course, there is no free lunch.

Margin Requirements

The margin requirement is a certain level of cash that you need to deposit in your margin account in order to sell a put option. There are three different ways that the amount required is calculated. The most frequently used method is known as the 25% rule. This is 25% of the stock price, added to the premium received for selling the option, less the amount that the option is determined to be out of the money. The 10% rule can also be used; this is 10% of the strike price, plus the premium you earn selling the option. The larger amount calculated by each method is used, and most of the time, it's going to be the 25% rule. In each case, multiply by 100 and then by the number of contracts you plan to sell, to get the total amount required to deposit in cash.

The margin requirement is like the collateral that you would deposit in your account with a put credit spread. Using a specific example, suppose that we are going to sell the $185 strike Facebook put option. First, we need 25% of the stock price, which is 0.25 x $189.71 = $47.43. The premium received for selling the option is $4.53. So, we add this to the stock price fraction to get $47.43 + $4.53 = $51.96. The option is out of the money by $189.71 - $185 = $4.71, and we can subtract this amount giving $47.25. Now you need to multiply this by 100 shares that underlie the option, giving a total of $4,725.

Selling two options a week would give us a weekly income of about $900, but we would need to deposit $9,450 in order to do it.

The cash requirements for selling credit spreads are lower, and the reason is that the option that you buy as a part of the deal mitigates your risk.

The Risk of Assignment

The risk when selling options is getting assigned, which means that you have a risk of having to buy or sell stock. Since most of the time, people sell put options, we will stick to that example. So, when you sell put options, there is a risk you will be required to buy shares of stock. When you sell a naked put option, you are stuck with the situation. You can, of course, sell the stock on the open market, but the risk is higher because the share price might drop low enough that you lose significant amounts of money.

But for the sake of example, let's suppose that Facebook had a bad earnings call, leading to a drop in share price to $175 a share, and you had foolishly sold the $185 put. In this case, the breakeven price is $180.47, so the option would be exercised, and you'd lose $5.47 a share. The way it would work is you would be forced to buy the shares at $185 a share. This would be mitigated by the fact that you had sold the option and gotten a credit of $4.53 per share. Now, you would have to sell the shares (assuming that you don't want them or are able to keep them) for

$175 a share on the open market. This is why a margin account is needed, so you can borrow the difference required to buy the shares. Remember that you only had to put up a few thousand dollars in order to sell the put option but buying 100 shares at $185 a share is going to cost you $18,500.

So how is a put credit spread different in this situation? Suppose that we sell a put credit spread with strike prices of $190 and $185. What happens then? The lower strike price is what you should buy, i.e., the $185 put credit spread. This means that we can sell the shares at that strike price. So, if the share price drops to $175 a share, we have some temporary pain when we are forced to buy the shares at $190 a share. However, rather than selling them on the open market, we would be able to sell them for $185 a share. Since the risk is mitigated by the second put option, we only have to deposit a few hundred dollars to act as collateral for the trade.

Deciding on what strategy to use is going to be a personal decision. Most high-level traders just sell naked options because of the simplicity, and they use their good judgment to pick strike prices that keep them in relative safety as far as having the option exercised.

Although you have to deposit more cash to sell naked options as compared to a credit spread, you can see that compared to a protected put, the amount of money required is quite small.

Naked Call Options

If you are in a situation where you expect the share price to stay below a specific value, then you can sell naked call options. Like naked put options, you have to have a margin account and deposit enough cash to cover the trade. Similar formulas are used. Unlike a covered call option, you don't need to buy shares in order to sell a naked call option. So rather than buying 100 shares of Facebook or whatever stock you are looking at, you will only have to deposit a few thousand dollars, and if you are using good judgment in choosing your strike price, you will be able to avoid having to buy the stock. In the event that you err and don't get out of the trade before the option is exercised, you will have to buy shares of stock on the open market and then sell them to the trader to exercises their rights under the option at the lower price. That means you will be taking a loss on the trade.

CHAPTER 19:

Analyzing Mood Swings in the Market

Modern markets are so volatile that a simple buy-and-hold strategy no longer has a place even for the long term.

The Market Is Uptrend

A bullish market is characterized by a succession of lower and higher points, and higher and higher points. In a clear uptrend, the corrective phases (drop legs) are less important in amplitude than the impulsive phases (legs of rising). This property is very important because it provides a valuable indication of the possibility of a trend reversal. When a corrective leg has a greater amplitude than the impulsive leg (bullish in a bull market), then the uptrend is likely to be challenged. The trader will have to reconsider the current trend and avoid positioning himself for the purchase under these conditions.

A downtrend market is characterized by lower and higher points, but also by lower and lower points. In this type of market, rebounds often have less amplitude than bearish legs, the main characteristic of a bear market. In a trending market, the movements that go in the direction of the dominant trend are still the most powerful. As for the uptrend, the turnaround can be anticipated. This requires the recovery to be larger than the last bearish wave.

The Market without Trend

In a trendless market, there is no clear trend, and low points and high points are often confused. Buyers and sellers are testing themselves and no clear consensus is at work.

According to Wilder, markets evolve in trend one-third of the time and do not draw any clear trend during the remaining two-thirds. This property is important because investors are often victims of momentum bias. They tend to prolong the recent course evolution mechanically. If the course progresses during the last sessions, they are convinced of the continuation of its rise and many traders are trapped by positioning themselves around resistance or slightly above2. Conversely, in the case of a decline in stock prices, investors say that this decline will continue and are trapped by opening a position around major support.

The good trader can wait patiently for the right moment before opening a position. Professional traders seek to position themselves at the beginning of an impulsive movement and avoid exposure by taking unnecessary risks when the market is not predictable. Good traders are people who can adapt to changing market conditions.

Trend Lines

Trend lines are often used by traders to identify bullish points in an uptrend and highs in a downtrend. In a bull market, the trend line goes through at least two low points. Conversely, in a downtrend market, the trend line will join at least two high points. It is possible to adjust trends over time based on new information: sharper, more marked trends may indeed appear as the trend initially traced becomes obsolete.

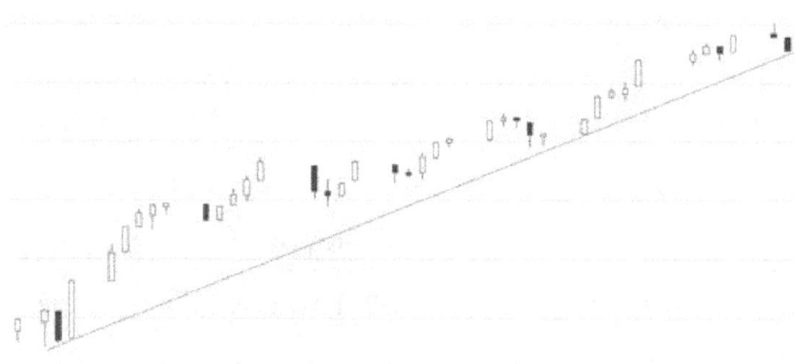

Conditions of Effectiveness of a Trend Line

The success of trend lines is justified by their effectiveness in identifying good levels of support and resistance. In other words, they sometimes make it possible to give with surprising precision these minor levels of reversal when a trend has already started. They also offer the possibility of identifying the state of the trend and anticipating reversals or simply corrective movements. In what follows, we try to give some elements to explain their effectiveness.

A first approach advances the argument of a stock market evolution respecting a "natural" phenomenon. There would exist on the market, and on all time horizons, trends that would respect a speed of progression and therefore a certain angle. The famous trader and analyst WD Gann explain that to last, a trend line must have a 45-degree angle. Not to mention natural phenomenon, we can say that a course of courses with a low slope indicates a slow movement that will probably abort. Conversely, when the slope is steep, the movement is too impulsive and will quickly run out of steam. The ideal is, therefore, to have an average slope (45 degrees), a sign of a healthy impulsive movement.

Another militant element in favor of trend lines is the fact that they are known to most operators. As we have seen, their validity will be strengthened because of the phenomenon of self-fulfilling prophecies. In concrete terms, a bullish trader will draw a trend line to identify the probable drop-off point for the stock, which will be a good buy with low risk. In the opposite case, it will draw a downtrend line to identify sales levels.

The importance of a trend line depends on the number of points it connects. The higher the number of rebounds on the right, the greater the importance. This is explained in particular by the mimicry of operators, which reinforces the strength of this line. In addition, the trend lines can be plotted over several time horizons (long, medium and short term), but the long-term trend lines or just to take them are those whose reliability is the most important. The trader will enjoy a return to the right of support (resistance) to strengthen its position buying (seller) and especially as the quality of the trend is proven.

Finding a Trend Reversal Using a Trend Line

Rupture of a trend line is an important reversal signal. This signal is all the stronger as the trend line is significant (it has been used on many occasions to support the current trend). The break of a bullish or bearish straight line materializes the end of a market dynamic: the operators who should have strengthened their positions near the trend line proved to be weaker than the opposing side (the bearers), thus allowing the rupture of the right and all the dynamics of the market. The change in trend thus seems clear.

A broken bullish straight line immediately becomes a line of resistance against which the market will crash; this is very often shown by a pullback (return to the right of a trend that has just been broken). The market thus tests the strength of the support that has become resistance (or vice versa). Beware; the break of a trend line cannot alone constitute a signal of a reversal of the market, as shown by the example of the title PPR. It only alerts the trader about the possibility of consolidation.

Canals or Channels

A channel (Canal) is a figure directly related to the analysis of trend lines studied previously. The tracking is simple: once a bullish trend has been determined, it is a question of finding a parallel to the tendency to cover all the evolution of prices. Over the period when the trend is observed (straight line connecting the extreme points), we thus obtain a channel in which the courses evolve harmoniously.

The channel will tuck into a trend by allowing impulse turning points to be determined through trend lines, but also corrective turning points through the upper channel of the uptrend channel - or the bottom line for a downtrend channel.

The courses thus vary between these two lines: the first constitutes the support line of the canal, where the courts come to rest; the second represents the resistance line of the channel (or top of the channel) against which the market stumbles.

As for trends, it is possible to distinguish short, medium and long-term channels. The importance of a channel depends on its duration of evolution, but also on the number of times each line of the channel has been affected. To be considered a canal, you need at least two impacts on each side. The higher the number of impacts, the more important the channel is.

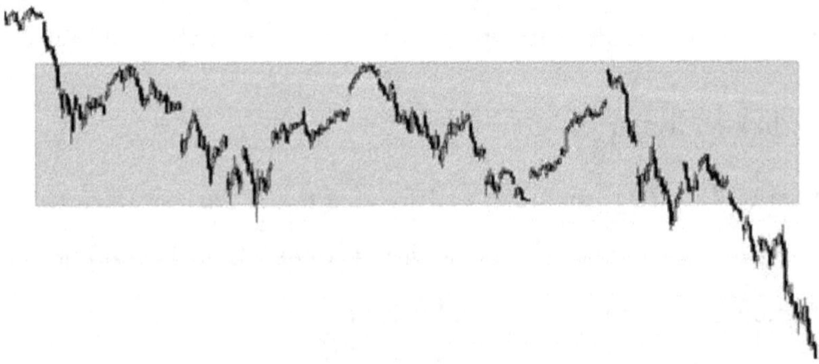

Intermediate Lines

In practice, prices do not move stubbornly between the lower bound and the upper bound. They sometimes have trouble passing intermediate areas within the canal. It is possible to draw parallel straight lines to the channel which constitute as many lines of support or minor resistance for the courses. However, the number of real intermediate rights is limited; one generally finds only one, even two. They are very often halfway through the channel and are real tests to know if the courses will reach the top or bottom. In the case of a bullish channel, the break in the intermediate resistance line often indicates that the market will reach the top of the channel.

It is also possible to distinguish within a channel small intermediate channels that allow, for example, the market to move from one terminal to another. Sometimes, too, a new channel emerges inside the canal, which appears more and more relevant, and which will eventually replace the old one that has become obsolete.

Rupture of the Canal

Two kinds of breaks can be envisaged: either the trend is confirmed and reinforced (it is an upward outflow of the uptrend channel or the decline of a downtrend channel), or it is reversed, and it is then a possible change of trend (downward release of a bullish channel and exit up a downtrend channel). The break is all the stronger as it is done in a large volume.

The operator has several elements to identify a possible rupture of the channel: in the case of a downward exit of a bullish channel, we usually notice that the courses have no strength, they do not arrive for example more to pass the intermediate right but stumble against it regularly. These elements are usually the first alarm signals.

Precautions When Detecting a Signal

The breaking of a bullish channel does not necessarily mean a sell signal, just as the break of a bearish channel does not always correspond to a buy signal. This is a simple indication that will need to be supported by other elements to become a relevant signal.

How to Detect the End of a Trend?

Can trend reversals be identified using chart analysis? We will see that it is possible to plot a reversal graphically, but for this, the trader will have to make sure that several criteria are respected: it is necessary to have a clear trend (for example, a trend line whose impulsive movements have a greater amplitude than corrective movements); the breaking of a major trend line or a major support is often a precursor signal of reversal; and finally, the various researches show that a figure of large turnaround (thus which took some time to be formed) will often be at the origin of an important corrective movement.

The Trend Reversal

After a downward movement (bullish), the title draws a bullish leg (bearish) whose amplitude is greater than the previous bearish (bullish) leg. This configuration signals a probable reversal of the trend and indicates the imminence of a bullish (bearish) departure or simply the cessation of the current trend and the entry of the market in a phase without a trend.

CHAPTER 20:

Trading for Long Term Profits

The Forex market is a tricky place to be without the relevant information. In order to become a successful trader, one needs to understand the charts and their way of working fully.

Trading to get long term profits is called longer-term position trading. This is different from the shorter-term scalping that is day trading. If you want to head in this direction, then it is imperative you get familiar with a few strategies to employ in order to achieve success.

The most important thing you need to know is that the amount of money you inject into this venture is not going to come back in a short time and you must, therefore, be very ready to make that investment.

This then calls for a good understanding of money and a great management formula for the money. If this is overlooked, then there will be a lot of wastage, and the lack of planning also makes it hard to accumulate the profits one might gain in the venture.

Another aspect that is often overlooked is keeping tabs with the market and having a reliable market analysis daily if not as oftentimes as possible during the day. This helps in letting one know what stocks are viable and their cost, variables in its pricing, and why you should choose a certain stock for long term profits.

Trading is most beneficial when it begins and ends on the same day, as is day trading. However, when you have looked at all your options and decided to venture for long term profits, the above are some of the considerations you should have before capitalizing on that.

Below are some benefits of trading

1. Source of income

Financial independence is the dream of every individual. Day trading can easily get you this freedom. A trader has the opportunity to trade as many times as they can in a single day. Depending on how well they are able to trade, they can earn huge profits from the trades that they engage in. The main trick in becoming a good investor depends on how well an investor can utilize the various option strategies to earn a source of income. For you to become an expert trader, you need to have some tactics that you can utilize. Those tactics set you apart from the novice traders. You might be wondering how you can get to this point while you are just getting started. Well, as a beginner, one of the core values you will require is the commitment to learn. Gaining knowledge makes you aware of what you are engaging in and makes it easier for you to become better at it.

2. Flexibility

We can discuss flexibility in two ways. The first way is the fact that you can trade anywhere at any preferred time and you can engage in any trade you would like.

How amazing would it be if you can earn money passively, without using much of your time and effort?

Most people do not get this, and that is why they make conclusions that option trading is a scam. Well, it is not as easy as it may seem. One has to use their mind and spend some time learning more about how it works. Once you get it right, it becomes easy for you. It is an investment that you can easily engage in and earn your profits at the end of the day as long as you know how to do it right. The other way is the fact that once a trader purchases an option, they have the opportunity to trade as many times as they can earn a profit.

These trades are conducted before the expiry date when the option contract is still valid. Depending on how well you utilize the option strategies, you can earn a lot.

3. Insurance

Options contracts can be utilized for insurance purposes. For a trader to use an option contract as insurance, they must build a good portfolio. Your portfolio indicates the profits an individual has made, together with the losses. A good portfolio needs to have more profits and fewer losses. As you trade, you need to ensure that you master the art of trading options.

This involves using the right trading plan and strategies to maximize your profits. Building a good portfolio is not a hard task. It is something that you can easily accomplish as long as you are committed to what you do. You keep getting better at it with every day that passes. In the beginning, you may encounter some challenges, but do not allow them to prevent you from getting where you would like to get. It is also important for you as a beginner to trust the process and believe that you will make it at the end of it all. Once you establish a good portfolio, you can use it as your insurance. It ensures that you do not acquire a complete loss, in case a trade goes contrary to what you expected.

4. Cost-effective

Different options contracts are priced differently. We have some that are more expensive than others. There are a number of factors that we have to consider when it comes to pricing options. Some of these factors include; the strike price, stock price, dividends, underlying asset, and the expiry date. When it comes to the expiry date, the options contracts that have a short period before they expire tend to have low prices. On the other hand, the options contracts, whose expiry date is quite far, tend to be highly-priced. As a beginner, you may find yourself opting to get cheaper options depending on your budget. Additionally, as a new investor, it is always good to start small. You may not be able to start with a huge investment at the beginning, especially if you have not tried it before. The beauty of investing in day trading is the fact that you can engage in any trade depending on your budget. You do not have to stretch beyond what you can afford. Any option can earn you a profit regardless of how it was priced; it all depends on your ability to earn from the options contracts.

5. Limited losses

The mistake most investors make is that they start trading with a lot of expectations. You think that you can make money within a short period of time, without having a strategy. I will disappoint you by telling you that it is impossible. You have to play your part in ensuring that you maximize your earnings as you minimize your losses. You cannot invest blindly and still expect an income at the end of the day. A lot of effort, commitment, and dedication will be needed. Most people miss this fact, and that is why they end up making losses. Once they have incurred the losses, they conclude that day trading is a scam. We have had a majority of the traders engage in overtrading only to end up losing every penny that they have invested. To avoid this, one has to be aware of the various option strategies. The different strategies are all aimed at increasing profits and reducing losses. This is easily achievable as long as one is committed to learning how each strategy works and when to utilize each best.

6. Limited risks

If you know much about investments, then you understand that most businesses, deals, or tradespeople engage in have risks. There is no single investment that an individual can engage in and fail to encounter risks. Day trading is no different from other investments. At times you will have to be open to the possibility of encountering some risks. These risks if not controlled can result in fewer profits or no profit at all.

Before engaging in a trade, evaluate all the possible risks. Get to know which you can afford to minimize as you leave aside those that you have no control over. This may seem like an easy task to undertake, but you need the right option strategy to do so. Depending on the type of trade you chose to undertake, you can easily get a suitable strategy to utilize. The strategy needs to be effective in minimizing the risks so you can earn more profits. As a trader, ensure you are well aware of all the option strategies that you can utilize in a trade. This knowledge allows you to make the right decisions while trading, and you easily earn profits as you reduce the potential risks.

7. Make huge profits

Every investor aspires to earn profits from the investments that they make. With day trading, you can make your dreams come true. One of the good things about day trading is that you can trade multiple times. As you engage in different trades, it is good to keenly observe what you do to ensure that you avoid making wrong decisions. Ensure that you evaluate all the trades that you engage in. This allows you to evaluate the possibility of incurring a loss or a profit. You get to know the trades that you can engage in and those that you need to avoid. As a beginner, avoid the trades with a high possibility of earning a loss and at the same time have a high possibility of earning huge profits. Such trade may seem to be good, especially if you lean on the possibility of earning huge profits. However, do not forget that both possibilities are applicable, and you can also make a huge loss. In such cases, you will be required to make the right decisions that can result in you earning profits.

You can also deal with multiple trades that earn small profits and get a huge profit at the end of the day.

8. Less commission

Less commission means that you earn more profits. While selecting the best brokerage account to use while trading, this is one of the factors you will have to consider. Ensure that the brokerage account has fewer commissions so you can increase your income. Different accounts have different rates for their services. As you do your research, you will come across some accounts with high commissions and those with low commissions. If you go to the accounts with high commissions, it will affect your profit. You will find that a percentage of your profits will be slashed and go into catering for the high commissions. The best thing to do would be to avoid such accounts and work with those that have low commission. As a beginner, you need to properly analyze all your choices to come up with the best solution. It is a good thing that with a single click, you can get all the information you would like from the internet. The reviews given in various brokerage accounts can also help you identify the various services that they provide and their rates.

CHAPTER 21:

Call vs Put Options Trading

In this field of text, we will discuss the difference between call option and put option.

Call Option Trade

Jacob is a farmer, and a cattle breeder who owns several dairy cows. Bob, who is an acquaintance of Jacob, is a trader of farm animals.

One day Bob gets a tip from a friend that the town's main dairy was negotiating a deal with a big international chocolate manufacturing company. If the deal were to materialize, the chocolate company would triple the quantity of milk they purchase from the dairy every day. To meet this increase in demand, the dairy would also have to increase milk production, and for increasing production, they would have to purchase many dairy cows at short notice. This move could result in a substantial increase in cow prices locally.

Bob realized he could make some excellent profits if he bought some cows from Jacob and then sold them after the prices went up. However, Bob wasn't entirely sure about this tip and did not want to buy cows upfront at the full price of $2,000 (which was the market price for a dairy cow at that time) and later sell out for a loss if the price did not rise as expected.

Therefore, Bob approaches Jacob and makes him a unique offer.

Bob tells Jacob that he will pay the latter a sum of $50 upfront for the right to buy one of his cows at the prevailing market price of $2,000, for the next 30 days. Also, Jacob would be under no obligation to return that amount if Bob no longer wanted to exercise his right (if cow prices dropped below $2,000).

Jacob saw no reason for cow prices rising anytime soon and was therefore glad to sign a contract to receive $50 from trader Bob in exchange for giving Bob the right to buy a cow at $2,000 for the next 30 days.

However, Jacob puts forth a condition that the proposed contract should cover 5 cows and not just 1 cow, and that meant Bob would have to pay $250 for the right to purchase 5 cows for a 30-day period.

Bob agrees to Jacob's condition, and therefore, Jacob pockets Bob's $250 and then signs the contract - the contract that gave Bob the right (but not the obligation) to buy 5 of Jacob's cows at the price of $2,000 for the next 30 days.

Bob knew that in the next 30 days, the market price of cows would either rise (as per his expectations), or continue to stay the same, or perhaps even fall (in the worst-case scenario).

If the market price for cows stayed the same at $2,000 or fell below that value in the next 30 days, Bob would have to give up the $250 he paid Jacob to get the agreement in place. Bob was under no obligation to buy cows at a lower price, and hence his losses will be curtailed to $250 only–the money he paid Jacob to sign the contract.

On the other hand, if the market price for cows went up within the next 30 days, Bob would approach Jacob to get 5 cows at $2,000 each and Jacob would be contractually obliged to sell the cows at $2,000, irrespective of how much more the cows were worth at that time.

Bob waits.

Three weeks after they put the contract in place, the town dairy signed a deal with the chocolate company to increase their daily supply of milk to the chocolate company by almost 4 times. To meet that demand, the dairy started purchasing many dairy cows at increasingly higher rates that resulted in the prices of dairy cows surging by almost 25% in the locality.

Following this price surge, Bob goes to Jacob and exercises his right to buy the 5 cows at $2,000 each. Bob then goes ahead and sells these cows to the dairy at $2,500 each.

Bob, thereby, makes a total profit of $2,250 for these 5 cows ($500 times 5 less the $250 for the contract amount he paid Jacob).

The trade that took place between Bob and Jacob represents how options trade works and if we apply stock market terms into the afore-mentioned scenario then:

A single cow represents one particular underlying Share/Stock. Bob is the Buyer of the contract, and Jacob is the Seller. Since this contract gives the buyer the right to buy–this contract is a Call Option.

$2,000 represents the Market Price of the share of the company (at the time they put the agreement in place).

$2,000 also represents the Strike-Price (SP) or the pre-determined price at which the proposed trade would take place between the buyer (Bob) and the seller (Jacob)–remember that Jacob paid $50 to purchase a cow at a fixed price of $2,000.

The $50 paid against each cow is called the Premium.

The number 5 shows the Lot Size of the contract–it is the fixed number of shares that an individual options contract covers.

Lastly, the 30 days in this scenario denotes the Time to Expiry of the options contract.

I hope you have entirely understood how a call option works now.

Put Option Trade

After being forced to sell 5 of his cows at a price lesser than the market price because of his contractual obligation, a slightly disappointed Jacob starts thinking.

From his experience, Jacob has seen that in situations where livestock prices increase sharply due to some change in the environment, the prices eventually come down marginally before reaching stability.

However, Jacob wasn't confident if cow prices had hit the ceiling yet–if he sold off his cows right away and prices continued to rise, he would miss a chance for selling at even better prices. The market price for a cow was $2,500, and Jacob wanted to wait for two weeks and see if it went up any further. If the prices were already at a high and if they dropped sharply, Jacob wanted to ensure that he could sell a few cows for at least $2,400.

Considering his predicament, Jacob gets into a contract similar to the one he had earlier signed with Bob. However, this time, he would be the 'buyer' of the right–the right to sell cows at a fixed price (unlike the right to buy that Bob purchased from him).

For this purpose, Jacob approaches Chad, a livestock trader in the local market, and offers him a deal. The deal was that, for the next 60 days, Jacob would have a right to sell Chad 10 cows at $2,400 each. And to own that right, Jacob would pay $30 per cow - a total of $300 for 10 cows.

Chad agrees and signs up for the deal and pockets the $300 since he didn't expect prices to fall from $2,500, let alone fall below $2,400. As long as cow prices stayed above $2,400 for the next 2 months (which Chad thought was very likely), he had nothing to lose.

A month and a half later, Jacob's prediction turned out to be right, and cow prices dropped to $2,250.

Therefore, Jacob goes to Chad and exercises his right to sell the cows at $2,400.

Since Chad was contractually obliged to buy the cows at $2,400, he has no choice but to buy the cows at the fixed price despite the cows being worth $150 less in the market. Jacob, thereby profits by $1200 ($150 x 10 less than the $300 paid for the contract) off his trade.

Like we did last time, let's apply the various stock market terms to this trade too:

A single cow represents one particular underlying Share/Stock.

Jacob is the Buyer of the contract while Chad is the Seller. Since this contract gives the buyer the right to sell–this contract is a Put Option.

$2,500 - the price of the cow, represents the Market Price of a share (at the time they put the agreement in place).

$2,400 represents the Strike-Price (SP) or the pre-determined price at which the proposed trade would take place between the Buyer (Jacob) and the Seller (Chad).

The $30 paid against each cow is the Premium.

The number 10 indicates the Lot Size of the contract.

Lastly, the 60 days in this scenario denotes the Time to Expiry of the options contract.

If you aren't still completely clear on the difference between call options and put options and all the various terms we have used so far. You want to go through these two examples one more time because you need to be completely thorough with your understanding of these trades to understand the strategies that will be taught.

CHAPTER 22:

Aggressive Options Trading

1. Writing covered calls

This is a strategy that is considered much safer than the outright purchase of stocks. It is generally referred to as CCW or covered call writing. It should be among the initial strategies to initiate as an intermediary trader. There are reasons why this approach makes sense.

1. The strategy is easy to understand:

With this strategy, you will simply sell your rights to purchase stocks at a specified strike price to another trader. After collecting the payment for the sale, you await the lifetime of the agreement to expire as it is limited. Should the buyer decline the opportunity to purchase the stock after the deadline, then your obligation to sell the shares will no longer exist.

2. Covered call writing provides plenty of beneficial trades compared to stocks purchase:

Basically, if the value of your stock declines, you will lose out less than a trader who does not have a covered call. You will also earn a profit when the stock price drops lower than the cost of the premium you collected.

Should the stock price remain mostly unchanged even upon expiration dates, then you will earn a profit while other investors such as those who buy stocks will only break even. You also earn more with the price of the underlying stock rise beyond the strike price at prices lower than the collected premium.

This profit is also higher than direct stock investors. If the related stocks experience a massive price increase, is the only situation where your earnings will be less compared to those of a buy and hold investor.

3. Covered call writing or CCW offers some protection, albeit limited, against any losses should the markets decline

Basically, when you collect money from the sale of the call option, you would have reduced the financial liability on the underlying stock.

What is a covered call?

We can define a covered call as basically an options trading strategy where you enter a long position in an underlying stock and then sell or write a call option based on the same stock. This is a strategy designed to generate multiple streams of income.

As an investor or trader, this is a strategy that you will use when you have a short-term neutral opinion on a particular stock. In such cases, an investor would hold-on to this position for a while, holding a short position while still earning an income. The term "buy-write" is another name used to refer to covered calls.

Covered calls – set up

The covered call strategy is considered a neutral strategy because traders mostly expect minimal rise or fall in the price of the underlying stock price for the entire life of the call option.

Basically, covered calls are not ideal for bullish traders or investors. Bullish traders should hold on to the stock rather than write a call option. The option will permanently cap the profit, and this will negatively affect the overall profit should the stock price go up.

Covered calls basically operate as a short-term hedge on a long position. This way, an investor or basically a trader gets to earn a profit from the profit received after selling the call. The challenge is that the investor will lose any gains the stock makes on the market. Also, if the call buyer decides to exercise their right to buy the shares, you will have to forfeit them.

This option strategy is also not suitable for very bearish investors. Such investors and traders should consider selling their stocks on the open market. This is because the premium received from selling the call option may not sustain losses incurred by a losing stock.

Best profit and loss scenarios

With a covered call option, the maximum profit that you can get is equal to the difference between the strike price of the short call option and the buying price of the underlying stock added to the premium obtained. The maximum loss will occur when the premium received is larger than the cost of the underlying asset.

How to write a covered call

First, select your preferred stock within your portfolio of shares, identify the stocks that you can be open to selling, and avoid those that you consider very bullish, especially in the long term. This way, you will not feel disappointed should you lose a stock which would otherwise have become profitable in the future.

Next, you should identify the strike price that you are comfortable with. This is the price at which you are happily selling the stock. The best approach to identifying the right strike price is to pick one that is out-of-the-money. The reason for this approach is because our aim is for the stock price to increase before it has to be sold.

After this, you need to choose the appropriate expiration date for the call option contract. The most ideal in this case would be one that is 30 to 45 days in the future. However, this is only a guide, so consider the dates carefully. The best date is actually the one that allows for a good premium when you sell the option at the chosen strike price.

2. Buying LEAP Calls as a stock substitute

Another great way of making money as an intermediate options trader is investing in long term calls, also known as LEAPS. The aim of buying long-term calls is to enjoy benefits that are the same as those that own the stock. However, buying the call option would limit your risk and exposure. In such a situation, the LEAP call will act as a substitute for your stock.

What are LEAPS?

We can define LEAPS as options that you buy for the long-term. They are considered a long-term investment that acts as a substitute for actually owning shares. In essence, you get to benefit from LEAPS as you would, if you own the underlying shares.

The acronym LEAPS stands for Long-term Equity Anticipation Securities. Generally, any stock options that have expiration dates more than 9 months are considered LEAPS. Such options are similar to other options, with the only difference being that they have a longer "life expectancy" compared to ordinary options.

The LEAP set up

Basically, if your thoughts on a given stock are bullish, then you can consider using the LEAPS arrangement. This way, a simple rise of about 50 points could translate to a rise of over 300%, which is highly profitable. Even then, there are risks involved, so it is crucial to be wary. Therefore, use caution and apply this strategy wisely. If you do so, then you will be able to leverage your investment considerably.

In most cases, LEAP stocks often have an expiration date beyond one year, while sometimes it is at least 9 months. This strategy allows you to invest a relatively small amount of money and buy options rather than spend larger amounts buying actual shares. Using this approach and strategy, you will be able to earn huge returns, especially if you make the correct decision regarding the movement of the shares.

How to get started

The first step in investing in LEAPS is identifying the appropriate stock for this strategy. Simply follow the standard procedure of purchasing a stock at the stock market. To determine the ideal stock for this strategy, you will need to do some research. There are websites where you can get useful information that will help with the analysis. Take, for instance, Ally Invest Quotes + Research. Do some fundamental analysis of the stocks until you find one that gives you enough confidence.

Once you determine the most suitable stock for this strategy, you will need to determine the strike price. Basically, you will need to invest in a deep-in-the-money stock option. This means a stock whose strike price is lower than the stock's current price. If you apply this strategy, then aim for a delta that is equivalent to or higher than 0.80 based on your chosen strike price.

This delta reference simply means that should the stock price go up by $1 your chosen stock option should rise by at least $0.80. The same reasoning applies if you select a stock whose delta is 0.95, which means that for a stock price increase of $1.0, then your stock option price will rise to $0.95. This is, however, theoretic. Anytime you use the Options Chains on Ally Invest, you will be able to see the deltas for each listed stock.

The starting point

When you want to invest in a LEAPS strategy, you should consider one in which the in-the-money stock price is 20% or higher. For instance, should the price of the underlying stock equal $100, then you should choose a call option whose strike price is lower or equal to $80 but not more. But if the stocks are volatile, then you should consider that it is even deeper in-the-money in order to acquire the kind of delta that you need. However, you should note that your option becomes costly should you go even deeper in-the-money. The reason is that the option gains a lot of intrinsic value even though the upside is a higher delta value. When your options have a higher delta, then the better they will serve as a stock substitute.

Expiration date

Always keep in mind that all options have an expiration date, including long-term options. Now, should the stock price ascend sharply after the expiration date, this will do you no good at all. Also, as this date approaches, most options tend to lose their value at a pretty fast rate. Therefore, you need to be extremely careful with these dates.

When it comes to this particular strategy of LEAPS, you should always opt for options that have at least a year to expiration. This is advisable as you will have sufficient time to benefit from stock movements in the course of the year without the burden or expense of actually buying the stock. Remember that in the end, this strategy is adapted for investment purposes where you want to make a large sum of cash rather than just a speculative tool.

Precautions when using LEAPS

One of the biggest precautions or risks when using this strategy is to use it as a risky gambling tool rather than the investment vehicle it was meant to be. For instance, some traders may select stock options with bad pricing or those that may probably never strike.

At other times it may be the case of piling risk upon risk by choosing long-term, less costly stocks for this strategy. Such options may not even fit into the definition of LEAPS because the expiration period may be less than 9 months. Sometimes traders make speculative trades and put themselves at high risk.

This strategy may not be suitable for all investors, so please approach it with care and understand the inherent risks involved. Pursue this strategy when you have the cash to spare and stocks that are just right. However, if you adopt the measures indicated and follow the right procedures, then you should be able to benefit immensely from this strategy.

CHAPTER 23:

Options Day Trading Styles

No matter what style or strategy an options day trader chooses to use, he or she needs to factor in three important components every single time. These elements are:

•Liquidity. This factor describes how quickly an option or other asset can be bought and sold without the current market price being affected. Liquid options are more desirable to an options day trader because they trade easier. Illiquid options create more resistance in the ease at which a trader can open or close his or her position. This extends the time needed to complete the transactions involved and thus can lead to a loss for the options day trader.

•Volatility. This describes how sensitive the assets attached to the options is to price changes due to external factors. Some assets are more volatile than others. Stocks and cryptocurrencies are volatile assets. Volatility has a great impact on an options day trader's profit margin.

•Volume. This describes the number of options being traded at a specific time interval. Volume is an indication of the associated assets price movement on the market because it is a gage of the asset's interest in the market. The higher the volume, the more desirable traders typically are in pursuing an option. Volume is one of the factors that make up open interest, which is the total number of active options. Active options have not been liquidated, exercised or assigned. If an options trader ignores taking action on options for too long, this can make circumstances unfavorable, which can lead to unnecessary losses. An options trader needs to always be on the ball about closing options positions at the appropriate time.

To take advantage of the options day trading choices listed below, the day trader needs to be very familiar with these factors and how he or she can use them to his or her advantage.

The Resistance Trading Strategy with Options

Breakout describes the process of entering the market when prices move out of their typical price range. For this style of trading to be successful, there needs to be an accompanying increase in volume. There is more than one type of breakout but we will discuss one of the most popular which is called support and resistance breakouts.

The support and resistance method describes the point at which the associated asset price stops decreasing (support) and the point at which the associated asset price stops increasing (resistance). The day trader will enter a long position if the associated asset price breaks above resistance. On the other hand, the options day trader will enter a short position if the associated asset breaks below the supported price. As you can see, the position that the trader takes depends on if the asset is supported or resisted at that new price level. As the asset transcends the normal price barrier, volatility typically increases. This usually results in the price of the associated asset moving in the direction of the breakout.

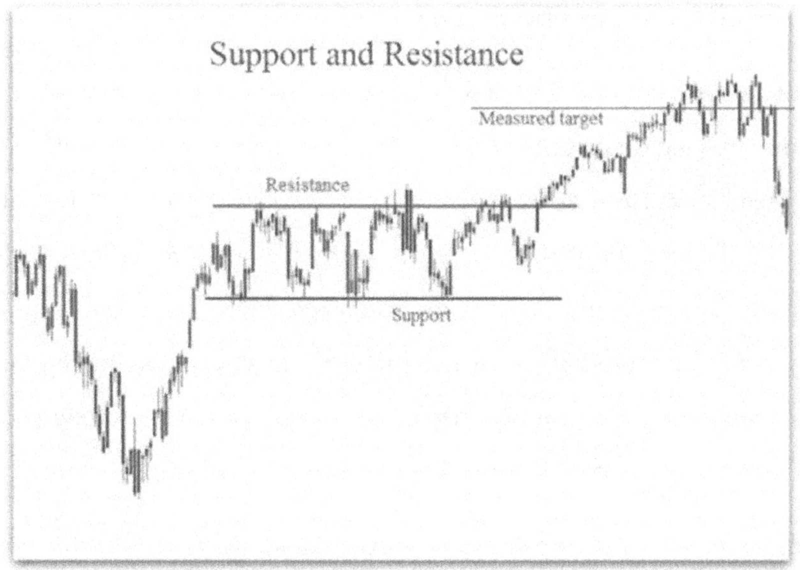

When contemplating this trading style, the options day trader needs to deliberate his or her entry points and exit strategies carefully. The typical entry strategy depends on whether or not the prices are set to close above the resistance level or below the support level. The day trader will take on a bearish position if this price is said to be above the resistance level. A bullish approach is a typical maneuver if prices are set to close below the support.

Exit strategies require a more sophisticated approach. The options day trader needs to consider past performance and use chart patterns to determine a price target to close his or her position. Once the target has been reached, the day trader can exit the trade and enjoy the profit earned.

Momentum Options Day Trading

This options day trading style describes the process of options day trading relying on price volatility and the rate of change of volume. It is so-called because the main idea behind the strategy is that the force behind the price movement of the associated asset is enough to sustain it in the same direction. This is because when an asset increases in price, it typically attracts investors, which drives the price even higher. Options day traders who use this style ride that momentum, and make a profit off the expected price movement.

This style is based on using technical analysis to track the price movement of the associated asset. This analysis gives the day trader an overall picture that includes momentum indicators like:

• The momentum indicator, which makes use of the most recent closing price of the associated asset to determine the strength of the price movement as a trend.

•The relative strength index (RSI), which is a comparison of profits and losses over a set period of time.

•Moving averages, which allows the day trader to see passed fluctuations to analyze the trends in the market.

•The stochastic oscillator, which is a comparison of the most recent closing prices of the associated asset over a specified period of time.

Momentum options day trading is highly effective and simple as long as it is done right. The day trader needs to keep abreast of the news and earnings reports to make informed decisions using this trading style.

What Is Reversal Trading and How this Works

This style relies on trading against the trend and is in essence, the opposite of momentum options day trading. Also called trend trading or pull back trending, it is performed when an options day trader is able to identify pullbacks against the current price movement trends. Clearly, this is a risky move but it can be quite profitable when the trade goes according to plan. Because of the depth of market knowledge and trading experience that is needed to perform this style effectively, it is not one that is recommended for beginners to practice.

This is a bullish approach to options trading and entails buying an out of the money call option as well as selling an out of the money put option. Both profit and loss are potentially unlimited.

Scalping Options Day Trading

This options day trading style refers to the process of buying and selling the same associated asset several times in the same day. This is profitable when there is extreme volatility on the market. The options day trader makes his profit by buying an options position at a lower price than selling it for a higher price or selling an options position at a higher price and buying it at a lower price depending on whether or not this is a call or a put option.

This style of options trading is extremely reliant on liquidity. Illiquid options should not be used with this style because the options day trader needs to be able to open and close these types of trades several times during the space of one day. Trading liquid options allow the day trader to gain maximum profitability when entering and exiting trades.

The typical strategy is to trade small several options during the course of the day to accumulate profit rather than trying to trade big infrequently. Trading big with this particular style can lead to huge losses in the space of only a few hours. This is why this style is only recommended for disciplined options day traders who are content with seeking small, repeated profits even though it is a less risky method compared to the others.

Due to the nature of this style, it is the shortest form of options day trading because it does not even last the whole day – only a few hours. Day traders who practice this style are known as scalpers. Technical analysis is required to assess the best bets with the price movement of the associated assets.

Scalping is an umbrella term that encompasses several different methods of scalping. There is time and sales scalping, whereby the day trader uses passed records of bought, sold and cancelled transactions to determine the best options to trade and when the best times for these transactions are. Other types of scalping involve the use of bars and charts for analysis of the way forward.

Using Pivot Points for Options Day Trading

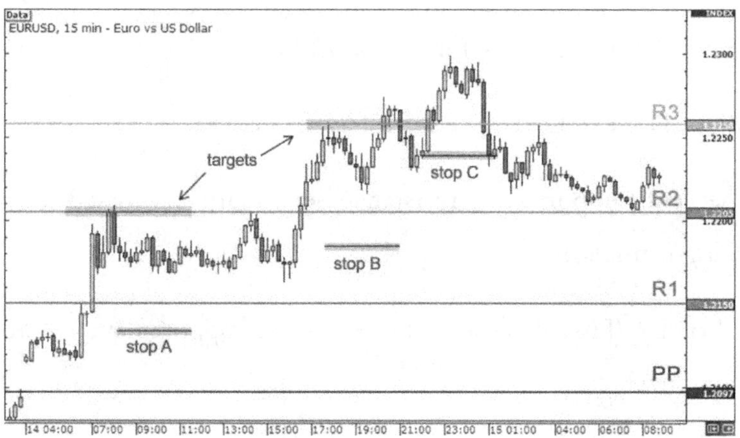

This options day trading style is particularly useful in the forex market. It describes the act of pivoting or reserving after a support or resistance level has been reached at the market price. It works in much the same way that it does with support and resistance breakouts.

The typical strategies with this particular options day trading style are:

- To buy the position if the support level is being approached then placing a stop just below that level.
- To sell the position if the resistance level is being approached then placing a stop just below that level.

To determine the point of pivot, the day trader will analyze the highs and lows of the previous day's trading and the closing prices of the previous day. This is calculated with this formula:

(High + Low + Close) / 3 = Pivot Point

Using the pivot point, the support and resistance levels can be calculated as well. The formulas for the first support and resistance levels are as follows:

(2 x Pivot Point) – High = First Support Level

(2 x Pivot Point) – Low = First Resistance Level

The second support and resistance levels are calculated with the following formulas:

Pivot Point – (First Resistance Level – First Support Level) = Second Support Level

Pivot Point + (First Resistance Level – First Support Level) = Second Resistance Level

The options trading range that is most profitable lies when the pivot point is between the first support and resistance levels.

The options day trader is vulnerable to sudden price movements with his style of trading. This can result in serious losses if it is not managed. To limit losses with this strategy, the options day trader can implement stops to marginalize losses. This is typically placed just above the recent high price close when the day trader has taken on a short position. This is placed just below a recent low when the day trader had taken on a long position. To be doubly safe, the options day trader can also place two stops, such as placing a physical stop at the most capital that he or she can afford to part with and another where an exit strategy is implemented.

Where these stops are placed is also dependent on volatility.

CHAPTER 24:

Best Rules for Day Trading

A higher percentage of individuals fail in day trading because of ignoring crucial rules. If you have made up your mind to do day trading, there are specific rules that you ought to follow to make huge profits.

Have a trading plan.

A trading plan is a set of guidelines that need to be followed by most traders to guide them in their activities. A trading plan helps you in proper money management to avoid losses. Before executing a trading plan, you need to back test and ensure it has positive results. Most of the trading brokers provide back testing tools in their software. A working and an affirmative trading plan will guide you on how to do your things the right way for you to succeed.

Set an entry and exit price.

To survive in this game, you ought to have knowledge of the entry plus that of exit prices. Day trading, like any other business, has worst-case scenarios. The entry price will help you understand when to get in while the exit point will help you to know when to get out. With the prices, you will able to plan yourself on how to handle things in terms of market disasters with no worries.

Do not rush to trade when the market opens.

Have a schedule for your trading. Do not rush to trade immediately when the market opens. These are risky moments since the trades might be of the previous nights, and the market is not stable at that moment. You should know the best time to make your trade. Different market securities have a different time to trade. Do not be overexcited and do things anyhow. Have a timing plan for your trades.

Have limit orders.

You are highly recommended to use limit orders in trading. What is a limit order? It is a trading order which gives you the capability to make sales and purchases in market trade at a specific price. Limit orders, unlike market orders, enable you to be in control of the maximum price you will pay for and also the minimum amount you will sell. A market order allows traders to purchase or sell orders at the current prices in the market.

A market order usually is concerned with the execution of the order made rather than the price. It will execute the order so fast with the current market price, unlike a limit order. A limit order checks on the amount and makes sure it is within the parameters of the limit order. If it does not fit within the settings, no trade executions will take place.

Shun from losses.

Losses usually are part of the game in all businesses but try your best to avoid them. Small losses are sometimes not a big deal, but watch out the losses not to be continuous. You might fail terribly. Be disciplined enough and follow your trading plan strictly. Learn the mistakes you make that lead to failures and correct them.

If the losses are still there, yet you followed your trading plan, change your strategies as quickly as possible or get out of trading. To be successful in trading, you need to cut off losses which will lower your profits.

Accept losses.

Losing in trading is part of learning. Do not panic when losses occur in trading; accept them. Learn from the failures and find a solution. Do not despair or anything. Even pro traders experienced losses once or twice and worked things out.

Take advantage of technology.

Day trading is all about competition. You should choose methods or techniques that are efficient for an excellent performance. You can implement some of the means by the use of modern technology tools in trading. The technology tools may include simple charting platforms and back testing tools.

Most of the charting platforms have simple user interface features that make it easier to read prices on the market. Back testing tools furthermore help traders to test their trading plans and strategies for better performance in trading.

Technology speeds up trading transactions and enables you to stay up to date. Staying up to date keeps you alert on any changes in the market like price fluctuations.

Be focused.

Being a focused and self-disciplined trader will save you from lots of trouble. If you want to be successful, get yourself together, have strategies and plans on how to do trading. Know when is the right time to make trades so as not to miss the golden time to do your trades. Having a schedule will keep you organized and managed. You have to follow this rule for success in day trading.

Trade with money you can afford to lose.

The risks involved in day trading are huge. The money to be used for day trading should not be capital or your savings which are essential aspects in all businesses.

You should instead trade along with cash specifically for trading, which will not be a big deal when you lose it and you can recover it so fast. Do not ever think of trading with your child school fees, you will be all messed up.

Manage your risks.

You need to have ways on how to handle your trading risks. Do not ignore them or else you want to be a failure in trading. Be familiar with the dangers or your day trading will be out of control. Make trades according to the trading plan and strategies, and you will ace it.

Have a mindset of steady growth.

You should possess a mindset of steady growth in day trading. Most of the traders have the mentality of getting higher profits all at once after starting day trading.

Rushing for huge benefits when you are not even stable will give you lots of stress. Relax, everything will work out well with time. Do the right thing at the right speed, and everything will eventually work out.

Avoid using margins.

Margins enable you to leverage your funds and even extra cash that you borrow from brokers. It can also increase your borrowing power. Operating on margins is sometimes risky in trading. Margins can increase or decrease in the market.

The significant risk involved in margins is its big loss that occurs when the margin falls. It makes it worse when you lose the funds that you have borrowed.

Have big goals.

You need to have stringent goals for yourself. Goals will assist you in working towards something that you need to accomplish. Visualize your goals so good and perform day trading towards them. Work hard and you will succeed in day trading.

Bear the business kind of mindset.

Businesses are involved with pretty much of things. They include profits, losses, expenses, risks, stress and so much more. Normally, it is highly recommended that that in-depth research about your business has to be undertaken and good strategies have to be laid so as to improve the potential of the business. Well, this is much similar to day trading, lay out a good plan with set strategies and learn more about your day to day trading occurrences in a bid to excel and acquire large chunks of profits.

A student of the markets.

Trading markets are quite dynamic. As a trader, you ought to discover what actually used to happen, what is happening and master all the facts involved in day trading as much as possible. This makes you really informed, educated and improves your rates of managing risks. With all these outcomes, undertaking day trading becomes quite easier and chances of incurring day to day losses become limited.

Developing and implementing the trading methodology.

A day trading methodology is a system of methods that are laid down so as the trader can implement them in their day to day trading activities. This discourages hesitation that is mostly experienced by most traders that just try out their luck during trading without any plan and really expect the best out of it. Day trading is not a "get rich overnight" kind of engagement but a certain activity that calls for intelligence and several tactical skills.

Frequently using stop losses.

A stop loss is basically a predetermined amount of risk that a day trader is willing to accept with each trade. It is normally in the form of a particular percentage or a certain trading amount, that limits the trader from exposure during trading. Most importantly, using stop losses ensure that risks and losses are limited.

Knowing when to stop trading.

There exist two reasons why you should most probably stop trading; the presence of an ineffective trading plan and an ineffective day trader. Major amounts of losses are expected in an ineffective trading plan probably due to the fact that markets may have changed, market volatility may have much lessened or perhaps the trading plan is just not working out as expected. This does not necessarily imply that trading has to be terminated, but the fact that a new trading plan had to be laid and strong trading strategies set.

On the other hand, an ineffective day trader is an unwanted day trader. So as to excel in day trading, there has to be a rule; be disciplined, follow your big plan, work hard and learn, be patient and so much on. If this does not entirely define you, then chances are that day trading is not really your kind of engagement.

Keep trading in perspective.

It is advisable to focus on the bigger picture during trading. Setting realistic goals is one of the ways of keeping trading in perspective. For instance, if a trader happens to have a smaller trading account, he or she should not expect some huge returns. Always work with what you have on your plate and really try to remain sensible. It is a step to step income-generating engagement that requires much patience and a variety of day trading skills. Also, winning and losing in day trading is really going to be such common events. When winning, enjoy and celebrate your good efforts but do not lose too much control and during the sad moments, remember that losing trade is not afar off. Stay put and focused.

Trading is not entertainment.

The word has been clearly misunderstood by most traders, especially beginners. The novice should realize that day trading is an income-generating engagement and also a capital diminishing kind of activity. Remember that failing to plan is also planning to fail. Plan your strategies, learn and get your day trading journey shining all the way with just a little loss occurrence.

Learn to trade options.

With trading options, a trader has to wait for a single day before money settles after a trade. The day trading options rules are T + 1. Read several blogs describing these and most preferably, check the kind that is not really advanced to avoid making it hard to implement several kinds of strategies at the early day trading stages.

Know the lingo.

Several terminologies need to be comprehended before you commence day trading. Some of them include:

Leverage: Increasing the money amount behind a given trade so as to maximize the possible returns created.

CHAPTER 25:

Trading Psychology of Investors

There are many qualities required for traders to be effective in the capital markets — the ability to grasp the economics of a business and the ability to evaluate the course of the stock price are two of them. Yet none of these analytical skills is as critical as the intellect of a trader: the capacity to control anger, thinks fast, and practice discipline — what we would call trading psychology.

The psychological dimension of trade is of the utmost significance. Traders also have to think quickly to make fast decisions, running in and out of markets in the short term. They need a clear strength of mind to do this. We do, by default, require consistency, so that we adhere to previously defined trading schedules and know when to book gains and losses. Emotions just can't get in the way.

Key Takeaways

- Market psychology refers to the dominant attitude of stock market investors at some moment in time.
- Investor sentiment will always push market performance in the direction of fundamentals.

- Learning what motivates fear and greed will give you the patience and objectivity required to be a good trader and take advantage of the emotions of others.

Understanding Fear

When traders hear negative news about a certain stock or the general economy, it's not uncommon to get frightened. They can overreact and feel obligated to liquidate their holdings and go to cash or refrain from taking any risks. If they do, certain defeats can be avoided, but gains can also be missed.

Traders need to realize what fear is: a rational response to what they see as a threat — in this situation, to their advantage or money-making ability. Quantifying fear could help, and traders should start talking about what they're afraid of and why they're afraid of it.

Through addressing this problem ahead of time and understanding how to respond or interpret those events automatically, a trader will expect to separate and recognize certain emotions during a trading session, and then seek to work on getting beyond the emotional reaction. This is not straightforward, of course, and can take place in reality, but it is important for the safety of the portfolio of investors.

Overcoming Greed

On Wall Street, there's an old saying, "Pigs get slaughtered." This adage applies to selfish investors who stay too long on winning bets, seeking to grab the last tick. Greed can be disastrous to recover, as a dealer is still at risk of being whipsawed or blown out of a spot.

Greed isn't easy to conquer. It's always founded on an impulse to try to do more, to try to get a bit more. The trader should learn to understand this impulse and build a trading strategy focused on sound business decisions, not on irrational impulses or potentially dangerous instincts.

Setting Rules

To keep their heads in the right position before they experience the psychological pinch, traders need to set up rules. They will set out rules based on their risk-reward appetite for when they enter a transaction and leave it — whether by a benefit goal or a loss stop — to keep sentiment out of the equation. In addition, a trader may decide to buy or sell security as a result of such factors, such as actual positive or negative earnings or macro-economic news.

Traders would also be smart to consider putting limits on how much they are able to win or lose in a day. Unless the income goal is met, they'll take the profits and run, and if losing trades exceed a set cap, they'll pack up their tent and go home, preventing more loses and surviving to trade another day.

Doing Research and Review

Traders should read as much as they can about their area of interest, teach themselves and, if possible, go to industry meetings and attend sales-side conferences. It also makes sense to prepare and commit as much time as possible to the testing process. This involves reviewing maps, talking to managers (if applicable), reading business papers, or doing other background work (such as macroeconomic analysis or market analysis) to speed up the start of the trading session. Information can help a trader overcome fear, so it's a useful tool.

In addition, it is vital that traders remain versatile and allow experimenting with new instruments from time to time. For starters, they may recommend using risk mitigation tools or setting stop losses at different locations. One of the best ways a trader can learn is through testing (within reason). Such experience may also help to reduce emotional effects. Finally, traders will regularly review their results. In addition to evaluating their returns and individual positions, traders will consider, among other issues, how they have planned for a trading session, how up-to-date they are on the markets, and how they are doing in terms of continuing education. This regular appraisal can help a trader correct mistakes and alter bad habits, which may help to improve their overall returns.

Fundamental Analysis

Fundamental analysis focuses on the cultural, social and political factors behind supply and demand. Many who use quantitative research as a market tool are looking at different macro-economic measures such as growth rates, interest levels, inflation and unemployment. Fundamental analysts must incorporate all this knowledge to determine current and potential results. It entails a great deal of effort and a detailed analysis, since there is no clear collection of values that direct fundamental research. Traders using fundamental research need to stay abreast of reports and developments on an ongoing basis, because they may signal future shifts in the cultural, social and political climate. Until investing, all traders will be aware of the general economic conditions. This is very essential for day traders who are attempting to make trading decisions on the basis of news reports, since while the Federal Reserve's monetary policy actions are still significant, if the rate change is fully placed on the market, the real reaction in EURUSD may be negligible. Taking a step back, currencies shift primarily on the basis of supply and demand. This is the most basic degree of currency rallying, as there is competition for the currency. If the market is for insurance, speculation or exchanging reasons, actual fluctuations are based on the need for a currency.

Currency prices should drop when there is surplus availability. Supply and demand will be the main determinants to forecast future revolutions. But how to forecast supply and demand is not as easy as anyone would imagine. There are several factors contributing to the overall supply and demand for a currency. It covers cash investments, export transactions, equity and hedge use. The US currency, for example, was very high (against the euro) between 1999 and the end of 2001. This rally was powered largely by the dot-com bubble and the willingness of international investors to share in such high returns. This demand for US assets allowed foreign investors to sell their local currency and buy US dollars. At the end of 2001, global instability has emerged, the United States has started to cut interest rates, and foreign buyers have started selling U.S. securities in search of better returns elsewhere. This allowed foreign buyers to sell US dollars, raise supply and reduce dollar value versus other global currency pairs. Availability of funding or investment in the purchasing of a currency is a crucial factor that can have an effect on the course of currency trade. It was one of the key generators of the U.S. currency between 2002 and 2005, making foreign official sales of U.S. securities (also known as the Treasury External Capital Exchange or TIC data) a significant economic measure.

Capital and Trade Flows

Capital flows and exchange flows are the balance of payments of a government, which quantifies the volume of demand for a currency for a given period of time. Theoretically, a balance of payments that equal to zero is necessary in order for the currency to retain its current value. A negative balance of payments statistic, on the other hand, implies that capital leaves the economy at a faster rate than it reaches and will thus decline in value.

This is especially important under current circumstances where the United States is running a chronically high trade deficit without any foreign investment to finance the deficit. As a consequence of this very issue, the trade-weighted dollar index plummeted by 22 per cent between 2003 and 2005. The Japanese yen is another clear example of this. As one of the biggest exporters in the world, Japan has a very strong trade surplus. Therefore, given a zero-interest rate strategy that prohibits capital flows from increasing, the yen inevitably continues to reduce demand on the basis of export flows, which is the other side of the equation. More precisely, a more comprehensive description of the scale of capital and trade movements follows.

Capital Flows

Capital flows measure the net amount of the currency that is purchased or sold on the basis of capital investment. A positive capital-flow balance ensures that international inflows of financial or portfolio investment in a country outweigh outflows. A negative capital-flow balance suggests that there are more tangible or portfolio assets made by domestic investors than by international investors. There are typically two types of capital flows — physical flows and stock flows (which are further segmented into equity and fixed-income markets).

Physical Flows

Physical flows include true foreign direct investment by companies, such as investment in real estate, manufacturing and local acquisitions. Both of these allow a foreign company to sell its local currency and buy foreign currency, which contributes to changes in the FX market. This is especially important for multinational mergers and corporate acquisitions requiring more cash than stocks.

Physical flows are important to watch, because they reflect the fundamental shifts in real physical investment activities. Such movements are changing in response to shifts in each country's financial health and development opportunities. Changes in local laws that facilitate international investment often foster physical movements. For example, as a result of China's entrance into the WTO, its foreign investment rules have been relaxed. As a result of China's affordable labor and lucrative sales prospects (over 1 billion people), multinational companies have overwhelmed China with investment. On the FX point of view, foreign companies need to sell their local currency and purchase Chinese renminbi (RMB) in order to finance investment in China.

Portfolio Flows in Equity Markets

When technology has made capital movement faster, trading in global equity markets has become much more feasible. Consequently, the revival of the stock market in any part of the world is an ideal opportunity for all, regardless of geographical location. As a result, a strong correlation has arisen between the country's equity markets and its currency: when the equity market is rising, investment dollars generally come in to seize the opportunity. Instead, declining equity markets may cause domestic investors to sell their shares to local publicly traded companies to take advantage of investment opportunities abroad.

CHAPTER 26:

Mistakes to avoid

Options trading is an entirely different animal as compared to normal stock market investing. Let's think for a moment about the common wisdom that is dispensed with regard to stock market investing. The general idea is to buy and hold, keeping your investments for a very long period of time. In fact, basically, you're expected to keep your investments until retirement. People do various strategies such as rebalancing their portfolio to match their goals, diversification, and dollar-cost averaging.

Options trading is a totally different way of looking at things. First of all, even if you are a day trader or engaging in activities like swing trading, the general goal, when it comes to stocks, is to buy when the price is at a relatively low point, and then sell at a high price. In reality, the day trader, the swing trader, and the buy-and-hold investor are no different. Buy-and-hold investors think that they are special and above everyone else, they are in reality just trying to make money off the stock market too. The only real difference, unless you are a dividend investor, is the time frame involved. So your buy-and-hold investor is going to hold the stocks for 25 years, and then they are going to start cashing them out for money. A swing trader makes money in the here and now.

So in that sense of options trading is more like swing trading. And in fact, in many cases, you're looking for the same price swings that the swing trader seeks. But as we've seen, options allow many strategies that are not available for any type of stock market investor. I suppose that in theory, you could buy huge numbers of shares of stock and try to set up similar arrangements, but it just wouldn't work. And besides that, even if it did it would require an enormous amount of capital.

The point of this discussion is just to lay out the groundwork and acknowledged that most of us come to options with a completely different mindset. So does take some getting used to and many beginning options traders are going to make mistakes. That's just the nature of the market because it's so different than what people are used to.

Going into a Trade Too Big

One of the mistakes that people make when they start out options trading is making their positions too big. Since our options don't cost all that much relative to the price for stocks, people aren't used to trading in small amounts. Even people who are not rich or anything thinking terms of the stock price and how much 100 shares with the cost. This can set up people for trouble. The temptation is going to be there to move on a large number of contracts when you start doing your trades, if you have the capital to purchase or sell them. This can actually get people into trouble. It's not really the dollar amount that's a concern, but it could get you in a position where you're not really ready to act as quickly as you might need to depend on the situation. So if you find trade and decide to sell 20 contracts, in the event that the trade goes south trying to buyback does 20 contracts might be problematic. Or you might end up buying a bunch of call options and have trouble getting out of them on the same day. It's actually better to have a few different small positions with the options than it is to have multiple positions when they are a large number. Remember that options prices move fast. You don't want to over-leverage your trades and be in a position where you can't find a buyer to pick up all 10 or 20 contracts.

Not Paying Attention to Expiration

This is probably one of the most common mistakes made by beginning traders. The expiration date is one of the most important factors that should be considered as you enter your trades. And once you've entered a trade, you need to have the expiration date of the options tattooed on your forehead.

This is something that is not amenable to being ignored. First of all, choosing the expiration date when entering the position is just as important as picking the strike price of the option. But one of the things that beginners do is to focus too much on the price of the option and the price-setting for the strike. The cost of the option and the strike price are obviously very important, the expiration date is important as well.

Unfortunately, far too many beginning traders ignore the expiration date when their trades are not working out. And so, they end up just letting the option expires. Of course, when that happens if it's out of the money, you are totally out of luck. It's just going to be at 100% loss. So, we need to be paying attention to expiration dates before we actually enter the trade, and we also need to pay attention expiration dates when we are managing the trade.

Buying Cheap Options

There is a saying that says you get what you pay for. There are reasons to buy out of the money options sometimes, but you shouldn't go too far out of the money. Unfortunately, many beginning traders are tempted to go far out of the money for the sake of buying a low-priced option.

The problem with these options is that even though out of the money options can make profits. If they're too far out of the money, they simply aren't going to see any action. So, there's no sense buying a cheap option just because you can pick it up for $25.

You don't want to be sinking your money into options where a massive price move would be necessary in order to earn any profits. It's fine to buy options that are near at the money.

Options that are close to being in the money can be very profitable even though they are out of the money. So, if you're looking to save a little bit of money when starting out your investing, that is always something to consider. But to make profits, the basic rule is there has to be some reasonable chance that's the stock prices going to move enough, in order to make the option you purchase going the money.

Failing to Close when Selling Options

If you want to remember just one thing from our discussion about selling options, whether it's selling put credit spreads or naked puts, you should keep in mind that it's always possible to exit the trade. The way that you exit the trade when you sell to open is you buy to close. You want to be careful about doing this because it's too easy to give in to your emotions and panic and prematurely exit a trade. However, you need to be aware at all times of the possibility of needing to close the trade. Riding out an option all the way to expiration is a foolish move unless it's very clear that it's going to expire out of the money.

As a part of this problem, new options traders often come to the market and they focus on hope as a strategy. When it comes to investing, hope is definitely not a strategy. Hope is something that belongs to a casino playing slot machine games. When you're training options, you should make as rational a decision as you can make it given the circumstances. So when the expiration date is closing and it's clear that the trade is not going to be profitable, don't give in to the temptation to say of waiting around for a reversal in direction. When you say something like that to yourself, that opens up the temptation to stay in the trade far too long. At some point, you might not be able to recover at all. So what you don't want to do, and this is true buying and selling, is hoping that there's going to be a turnaround and waiting to see what happens.

For those who are buying options to open their positions, this is the worst of all possible strategies. Remember that when you buy to open a position, time decay is working against you at all times. So unless the stock is moving in a good direction, there isn't a reason to hold the option. For sellers, time decay actually works in your favor. But there can be situations when it's just smart to get out of the trade. Let's look at a couple of examples.

If you sell to open an iron condor, and for some reason, the stock has a breakout to one direction or the other, it's better to get out of the iron Condor now. We aren't talking about a one or two dollar change. If the stock goes in such a direction that one of your options goes in the money by a small amount, that type of trade is worth waiting out to see what happens. But if there is a big break to the upside or the downside, it would be foolish to stay in the trade. For one thing, there would be at risk of assignment, but the most likely situation is that you're just going to lose the maximum amount of money. But if you have a good strategy and only getting involved with options that have a high level of open interest, almost no matter what the situation is, you should be able to buy and sell that option pretty quickly.

The other obvious example is if you were selling a put credit spread already naked put, and you noticed that the share price is declining right towards your strike price. You don't have to panic right away because remember that in order for exercising the option to be worthwhile, the share price has to move enough, so that not only does the option go in the money, but the price move also accounts for the money that was paid for the premium to buy the contract. So, if you have a strike price of $100 and someone paid two dollars to buy the option, if the share price is $99, they are going to exercise the option. Even if it drops to

$98, they still might not exercise the option, unless there was some factor to indicate that the stock was about to turn around so they can sell it at a profit. But that's an unlikely scenario. It's only when it starts going strong and that there's a problem.

CHAPTER 27:

Tips, Tricks and Suggestions to Excel

- Know when to go off book: While sticking to your plan, even when your emotions are telling you to ignore it, is the mark of a successful trader, this in no way means that you must blindly follow your plan 100 percent of the time. You will, without a doubt, find yourself in a situation from time to time where your plan is going to be rendered completely useless by something outside of your control. You need to be aware enough of your plan's weaknesses, as well as changing market conditions, to know when following your predetermined course of action is going to lead to failure instead of success. Knowing when the situation really is changing, versus when your emotions are trying to hold sway is something that will come with practice, but even being aware of the disparity is a huge step in the right direction.

- Avoid trades that are out of the money: While there are a few strategies out there that make it a point of picking up options that are currently out of the money, you can rest assured that they are most certainly the exception, not the rule. Remember, the options market is not like the traditional stock market which means that even if you are trading options based on underlying stocks buying low and selling high is just not a viable strategy. If a call has dropped out of the money, there is generally less than a 10 percent chance that it will return to acceptable levels before it expires which means that if you purchase these types of options what you are doing is little better than gambling, and you can find ways to gamble with odds in your favor of much higher than 10 percent.

- Avoid hanging on too tightly to your starter strategy: Your core trading strategy is one that should always be constantly evolving as the circumstances surrounding your trading habits change and evolve as well. What's more, outside of your primary strategy you are going to want to eventually create additional plans that are more specifically tailored to various market states or specific strategies that are only useful in a narrow band of situations. Remember, the more prepared you are prior to starting a day's worth of trading, the greater your overall profit level is likely to be, it is as simple as that.

- Utilize the spread: If you are not entirely risk averse, then when it comes to taking advantage of volatile trades the best thing to do is utilize a spread as a way of both safeguarding your existing investments and, at the same time, making a profit. To utilize a long spread, you are going to want to generate a call and a put, both with the same underlying asset, expiration details, and share amounts but with two very different strike prices. The call will need to have a higher strike price and will mark the upper limit of your profits and the put will have a lower strike price that will mark the lower limit of your losses. When creating a spread, it is important that you purchase both halves at the same time as doing it in fits and spurts can add extraneous variables to the formula that are difficult to adjust for properly.

- Never proceed without knowing the mood of the market: While using a personalized trading plan is always the right choice, having one doesn't change the fact that it is extremely important to consider the mood of the market before moving forward with the day's trades. First and foremost, it is important to keep in mind that the collective will of all of the traders who are currently participating in the market is just as much as a force as anything that is more concrete, including market news. In fact, even if companies release good news to various outlets and the news is not quite as good as everyone was anticipating it to be then related prices can still decrease.

- Never get started without a clear plan for entry and exit: While finding your first set of entry/exit points can be difficult without experience to guide you, it is extremely important that you have them locked down prior to starting trading, even if the stakes are relatively low. Unless you are extremely lucky, starting without a clear idea of the playing field is going to do little but lose your money. If you aren't sure about what limits you should set, start with a generalized pair of points and work to fine tune it from there.

- Never double down: When they are caught up in the heat of the moment, many new options traders will find themselves in a scenario where the best way to recoup a serious loss is to double down on the underlying stock in question at its newest, significantly lowered, price in an effort to make a profit under the assumption that things are going to turn around and then continue to do so to the point that everything is completely profitable once again. While it can be difficult to let an underlying stock that was once extremely profitable go, doubling down is rarely if ever going to be the correct decision. If you find yourself in a spot where you don't know if the trade you are about to make is actually going to be a good choice, all you need to do is ask yourself if you would make the same one if you were going into the situation blind, the answer should tell you all you need to know.

- Never take anything personally: It is human nature to build stories around, and therefore form relationships with, all manner of inanimate objects including individual stocks or currency pairs. This is why it is perfectly natural to feel a closer connection to particular trades, and possibly even consider throwing out your plan when one of them takes an unexpected dive. Thinking about and acting on are two very different things, however, which is why being aware of these tendencies are so important to avoid them at all costs.

Not taking your choice of broker seriously: With so many things to consider, it is easy to understand why many new option traders simply settle on the first broker that they find and go about their business from there. The fact of the matter is, however, that the broker you choose is going to be a huge part of your overall trading experience which means that the importance of choosing the right one should not be discounted if you are hoping for the best experience possible. This means that the first thing that you are going to want to do is to dig past the friendly exterior of their website and get to the meat and potatoes of what it is they truly offer. Remember, creating an eye-catching website is easy, filling it will legitimate information when you have ill intent is much more difficult. First things first, this means looking into their history of customer service as a way of not only ensuring that they treat their customers in the right way, but also of checking to see that quality of service is where it needs to be as well. Remember, when you make a trade every second count which mean that if you need to contact your broker for help with a trade you need to know that you are going to be speaking with a person who can solve your problem as quickly as possible. The best way to ensure the customer service is up to snuff is to give them a call and see how long it takes for them to get back to you. If you wait more than a single business day, take your business elsewhere as if they are this disinterested in a new client, consider what the service is going to be like when they already have you right where they want you. With that out the way, the next thing you will need to consider is the fees that the broker is going to charge in exchange for their services. There is very little regulation when it comes to these fees which means it is definitely going to pay to shop around. In addition to fees, it is important to consider any account minimums that are required as well as any fees having to do with withdrawing funds from the account.

Find a Mentor: When you are looking to go from causal trader to someone who trades successfully on the regular, there is only so much you can learn by yourself before you need a truly objective eye to ensure you are proceeding appropriately. This person can either be someone you know in real life, or it can take the form of one or more people online. The point is you need to find another person or two who you can bounce ideas off of and whose experience you can benefit from. Options trading doesn't need to be a solitary activity; take advantage of any community you can find.

Knowledge is the key: Without some type of information which you can use to assess your trades, you are basically playing at the roulette table. Even poker players show up to the table with a game plan. They can adapt to the circumstances and learn to read other players. That way, they can tell the contenders from the pretenders. Options trading is no different. If you are unable to use the information that is out there to your advantage, then what you will end up with is a series of guesses which may or may not play out. Based purely on the law of averages you have a 50/50 chance of making money. That may not seem like bad odds, but a string of poor decisions will leave you in the poor house in no time. So, it is crucial that you become familiar with the various analytics and tools out there which you can use to your advantage. Bear in mind that everyone is going to be looking at the same information. However, it is up to you to figure out what can, or might, happen before everyone else does. This implies really learning and studying the numbers so that you can detect patterns and see where trends are headed, or where trends may reverse. The perfect antidote to that is vision and foresight. Practice building scenarios. Try to imagine what could happen is trends continue. Or, what would happen if trends reversed? What needs to happen in order for those trends to continue or reverse? When you ask yourself such tough questions, your knowledge and understanding begin to expand. Your mind will suddenly be able to process greater amounts of information while you generate your own contingency plans based on the multiple what ifs. That may seem like a great deal of information to handle, but at the end of the day, any time spent in improving your trading acumen is certainly worth the effort.

CHAPTER 28:

An Example of Trade

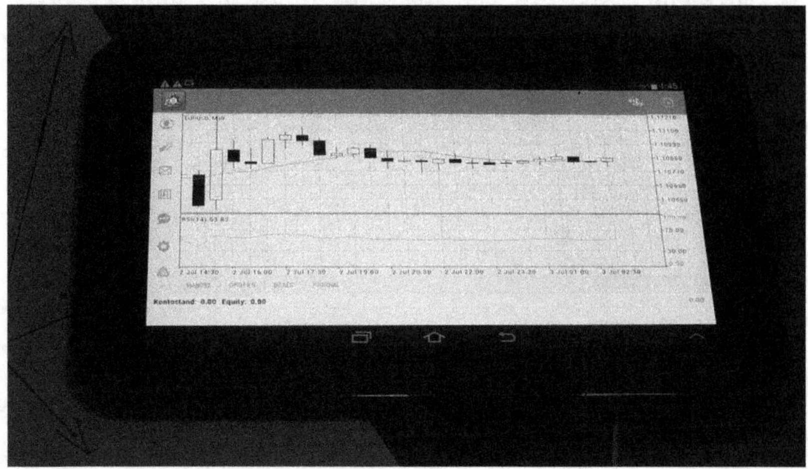

The investment in the medium and long-term is ideal for those who want to build capital, or simply diversify and enhance savings over time simply and at reduced costs. Given their versatility, ETFs can be used in different medium and long-term investment strategies, where they can support or replace traditional instruments, thus allowing to achieve the set objective. Currently, the range of ETFs is so diverse that any FCI can be replicated (at a much higher cost)

A strategy to invest its capital in the medium to long term is to resort to investment funds, whose popularity has grown progressively over the last twenty years. One of the main characteristics of the Funds is that of allowing the underwriter to enter the market with modest capital and to obtain professional management that will allow them to obtain positive results over time, with moderate risk. Investment funds should favor more active management, even if this does not always happen. In addition to weighing on their final return, they are the highest management costs to which the same funds are subject, and whose impact is felt particularly in times of slowdown or stagnation of the market. In light of this situation, the investor could find it convenient to substitute the investment in funds with that of ETFs that aim to follow closely the evolution of its benchmark index, while offering the maximum possible transparency.

In advance it cannot be said whether it is better to invest in funds or in ETF; to make this choice you have to decide if you want the manager to move away from the benchmark (and from which benchmark): this possibility is called "active risk." Active risk is not necessarily bad, because there are some managers who are actually better than others, but in reality, they are few and, not always, you can find them. If you decide to move away from the basic risk, you must be convinced that:

good managers exist;

that they can do better than their benchmark;

above all, be able to find them!

If you think you can complete each of the three phases, it is appropriate to rely on active funds, otherwise, ETFs are preferred because they cost less and carry precisely where you decided to go, without additional surprises.

The techniques for choosing the ETF that best suits your investment strategies are different; an interesting methodology is applied to sector rotation: the market as a whole is made up of different equity sectors, corresponding to the different economic sectors and their continuous alternation from the origin to the expansion and contraction phases. For this reason, the moments in which all the economic sectors grow or decrease simultaneously are quite rare. The concept of sector rotation is useful to identify, on the one hand, the stage of maturity of the current primary trend and on the other to select those sectors that have a growing relative strength. For example, sectors sensitive to changes in interest rates tend to anticipate both the minimums and the maximums of the market, while the sectors sensitive to the demand for capital goods or raw materials generally tend to follow the overall trend of the market with delay. Through ETFs, it is possible to take an immediate position on a specific stock, without necessarily being forced to buy the different securities belonging to that particular basket. In this way, it will be possible to obtain immediate exposure to this sector, benefiting at the same time as its growth in value, besides the advantages linked to the diversification.

It is also possible to invest using relative strength, investing, perhaps, on a stock exchange index, at the same time benefiting from its growth in value, in addition to the advantages linked to diversification.

For example, if one thinks that at a given moment the US market should grow in relative terms to a greater extent than the French one, it will be appropriate to make the first one and to underweight the second one. This decision can be reached by analyzing the comparative relative strength between the two markets, which compares two dimensions (composed of market, sector, securities or other indices) to show how these values are performing in a relative manner. Respect to each other. The trend changes expressed by relative strength generally tend to anticipate the actual ones of the financial activity to which it refers. It is, therefore, possible to use the relative strength to direct purchases towards ETFs that show a growing relative force.

The great flexibility of ETFs also allows the construction of guaranteed capital investment; in times of financial turbulence, investors often turn to products that provide capital protection: those provided by financial intermediaries often have high fees and charges for customers. Not many people know that it is possible to build a guaranteed capital product by yourself, which respects your personal investment needs! The central point of the logic of guaranteed capital is interest rates and the duration of the investment because at the base of all there are the two central concepts of finance:

The higher the interest rates, the greater the return on the money as the duration increases, you earn more, because money "works" longer

The money we will obtain in many years can be brought to today, as for bills that follow the discount law (the technical term of bringing the future money to today). You can easily answer the question: "to have

100 euros in seven years, knowing that the rates are at 5%, how much money do I have to invest?" This statement indicates how much money is needed to invest today to get the desired amount at maturity. The bonds that allow only the fruits to maturity, without paying interest during their life, are called zero-coupon bonds (zcb) and are quite common on the market. If for example, I want to have € 100 at maturity and interest rates are at 5% I will have to invest in zero-coupon bonds € 95.24 (if the deadline is between 1 year) € 78.35 (if the deadline is in 5 years) € 61.39 (if the deadline is 10 years) 48.1 € (if the deadline is between 15 years) and 23.21 € (if the deadline is 30 years)

In effect, by building investment with guaranteed capital, one only has to decide how to invest the remaining part of the initial 100 euros that have not been allocated in the zero coupons. An ideal solution could be to invest in options because, thanks to the leverage effect, they can amplify any yield. If you have a less aggressive investment profile, ETFs are excellent tools to build guaranteed capital investment. If, for example, we assume a 10-year investment with rates of 2.5% for that maturity, the portion to be invested in zcb is equal to 78.12%, while the remaining 21.88% will be invested in ETF.

This investment strategy makes it possible to achieve a minimum (not real) "money" return target with few operations, as the zcb provides for the repayment only on the nominal amount of the loan (not discounted to the inflation rate). It is, therefore, a valid methodology for those who intend to make investments with clear objectives and have little time to devote to monitoring the values as only an operation until expiry may be necessary. Unlike a guaranteed capital product offered by any financial intermediary, an investment of this kind built independently with ETFs can be dismantled entirely or in pieces (selling only the zcb or active assets, ETF) to meet any need. Naturally, only at maturity will there be a certainty of the pre-established return and, over the course of the loan, a temporary adverse trend in financial variables, (rates rise by lowering the zcb and at the same time decreasing the value of the ETF) could result in the liquidation of losing positions. The same consequence would be selling a structured bond, with the advantage that "doing it at home" the commissions are much lower and you can separate the two components and, if necessary, liquidate only one, according to specific needs.

Profitability of equity (Roe): this is the ratio between the net result and the net assets of a given company, in particular from the point of view of equity investments is an important parameter as a profitability higher than the cost of capital is an index of the ability of an enterprise to create value, therefore it should be a guarantee of greater capacity for growth of the securities in the phases of the rise of the market and of resistance in the reflexive phases. From this point of view, the Roe is always held in strong consideration by those who choose to invest in shares today.

Price/earnings ratio: a low ratio of this parameter makes a share price particularly attractive, but at the same time it could mean that expectations regarding future profits are not particularly positive. As in the case of the Roe, this is a factor to be taken into due consideration when choosing the best actions to invest in.

Price-book value ratio: the ratio between the share price and the net asset value resulting from the last balance sheet, especially if this ratio is lower than the unit means that the company is being paid less than the value of the budget net of liabilities. However, this does not necessarily mean that it is a good deal, since the company may not be able to produce profits either.

Dividend yield: this is the percentage ratio between the last distributed dividend and the share price, in particular, it measures the remuneration provided by the company to shareholders in the last year in the form of liquidity. This parameter is often taken into account to identify the securities to invest in, since a company able to distribute dividends is generally a healthy company, but also in this case, as with all the other selection parameters, it is necessary to a broader and more complete analysis, since a high level of this indicator could also mean that the company has made few investments or has little prospect of growth. For this reason, looking at the dividend yield as a primary factor in determining the securities in which to invest in the options market is reductive. The dividend yield only makes sense if accompanied by considerations on any business plans and industrial plans of the listed company. Only in this way is it possible to have guarantees on what are the prospects of the group in the future.

Rating and target price: the rating is the judgment that certain analysts and investment banks have on a specifically listed security while the target price represents the maximum target price to which the security may go. Dozens of judgments are published daily on all listed shares.

Conclusion

First of all, we would point out that the whole guide was written without relying on any kind of fees. As we already mentioned, fees vary, and every brokerage house has its own rules about it.

· Trading options have significant risks. If you are absolutely inexperienced with trading, we would recommend talking with a financial advisor before making any decision.

· Always keep in mind that every investment has its own risk and reward rating which means that if the risk is high, the reward will be high too.

· Expiration date of American style options and European style options (the most commonly used ones) is always the third Saturday in the month for American and the last Friday before the third Saturday for European options.

· Phrase "in the money" describes that the option has a value higher than the strike price for call options and lower than the strike price for put options at the time of their expiration.

· The most common minimal bid for option sharing is one nickel or 5 dollars per contract. However, some more liquid contracts allow minimal bid to be one dollar per contract.

· 100 shares of the certain stock are actually 1 option contract

· If you pay 1 dollar for an option your premium for that option whether you buy or sell it is 1 dollar per share, which means that the option premium is 100 dollars per contract

· All of the examples in this guide assume that every option order ever mentioned was filled successfully.

· Whenever you want to open a new position you will have to sell or buy on the market to "open". The same principle applies if you wish to close your position. You sell or buy to "close".

· Phrase Open Interest represents the number of option contracts that are opened at the moment. Logically- more opened contracts mean a bigger number and closed contracts mean a smaller number.

· Volume of the options is the number of contracts that are traded in one single day.

Be careful when signing the contracts; make sure you read all of the trading options.

So here we are at the end of this guidebook on trading options. They can be extremely profitable but learning to trade them well takes time. You can choose to use indicators to determine your entry points, and I'm all for this approach at first but remember that over the long term, you're better served learning the basics of order flow and using that.

There is no shortage of options strategies you can use to limit your risk and depending on the volatility levels dramatically, you can deploy separate strategies to achieve the same ends. Contrast this with a directional trading strategy where you have just one method of entry, which is to either go short or go long, and only one way of managing risk, which is to use a stop loss.

Spread or market neutral trading puts you in the position of not having to care about what the market does. In addition, it brings another dimension of the market into focus, which is volatility. Volatility is the greatest thing for your gains and options allow you to take full advantage of this, no matter what the volatility situation currently is.

Options can be a bit hard to get your head around at first since so many of us are used to looking at the market as a thing that goes up or down. Options bring a sideways and a different vertical element to it via spreads and volatility estimates. More advanced options strategies take full advantage of volatility and are more math-focused, so if this interests you, you should go for them.

That being said, do not assume the complexity means more gains. The strategies shown here are quite simple, and they will make you money thanks to the way options are structured. They bring you the advantage of leverage without having to borrow a single cent.

You can choose to borrow, of course, but you need to do this only if it is in line with your risk management math. Risk management is what will make or break your results and at the center of quantitative risk management is your risk per trade. Keep this consistent and line up your success rate and reward to risk ratios, and you'll make money as a mathematical certainty.

Qualitative risk management requires you to adopt the right mindset with regards to trading, and it is crucial for you to adopt this as quickly as possible. Remember that the implications of your risk math mean that you need not be concerned with the outcome of a single trade. Instead, seek to maximize your gains over the long term.

The learning curve might get steep at times, but given the rewards on offer, this is a small price to pay. Keep hammering away at your skills, and soon you'll find yourself trading options profitably, and everything will be worth it. How much can you expect to make trading options?

Generally, a good options trade can expect around 50-80% returns on their capital. As you grow in size, this return amount will decrease naturally. However, to start off with these are beyond excellent returns.

Always make sure you're well capitalized since this is the downfall of many traders. You need to be patient with the process. A lot of people rush headfirst into the market without adequate capitalization or learning and soon find that the markets are far tougher than they thought. So always ensure the mental stress you place yourself in is low and that you're never in a position where you 'have' to make money trading.

I wish you the best of luck in all of your trading efforts. The key to success is to simply never give up and to be resilient. Reduce the stress on yourself, and you'll be fine. Here's wishing you all the success in your options trading journey!

CPSIA information can be obtained
at www.ICGtesting.com
Printed in the USA
BVHW040934300421
605946BV00016B/469